ONCE UPON A RHYME

IMAGINATION FOR A NEW GENERATION

Devon & Cornwall Vol II

Edited by Natalie Catterick

Young Writers

First published in Great Britain in 2004 by:
Young Writers
Remus House
Coltsfoot Drive
Peterborough
PE2 9JX
Telephone: 01733 890066
Website: www.youngwriters.co.uk

SB ISBN 1 84460 588 4

Foreword

Young Writers was established in 1991 and has been passionately devoted to the promotion of reading and writing in children and young adults ever since. The quest continues today. Young Writers remains as committed to engendering the fostering of burgeoning poetic and literary talent as ever.

This year's Young Writers competition has proven as vibrant and dynamic as ever and we are delighted to present a showcase of the best poetry from across the UK. Each poem has been carefully selected from a wealth of *Once Upon A Rhyme* entries before ultimately being published in this, our twelfth primary school poetry series.

Once again, we have been supremely impressed by the overall high quality of the entries we have received. The imagination, energy and creativity which has gone into each young writer's entry made choosing the best poems a challenging and often difficult but ultimately hugely rewarding task - the general high standard of the work submitted amply vindicating this opportunity to bring their poetry to a larger appreciative audience.

We sincerely hope you are pleased with our final selection and that you will enjoy *Once Upon A Rhyme Devon & Cornwall Vol II* for many years to come.

Contents

Esther Seaford (9)   38
Melissa Warner (9)   38
Bridget Suzanne Phillips (8)   39
Luke Pedlar (9)   39
Matthew Newton (9)   39

Hazeldown Primary School
Katherine Stone (10)   40
Emma Roby (11)   40
Matthew Rushton (11)   41
Hannah Holliday (11)   41
James Treweek (11)   42
Emma Lane (10)   42
Maria Bykova (11)   43
Megan Thomson, Eve Sydenham,
                    Charlotte L & Maddie W (11)   43
Alice Smiddy (11)   44
Jack Kelly Stacey (11)   45

Manadon Vale Primary School
Abigail Jopson (8)   45
Hannah French (8)   46
Joshua Edwards (8)   46
Scott Hardman (8)   47
Samuel Couch (7)   47
Haaris Khan (8)   48
Andrew Pond (8)   48
Liam Lewis (8)   49
Amy Gumbrell (8)   49
Kirsten Masters (7)   50
Daniel Jones (8)   50
Joseph Weinling (8)   51
Zacharias Evans (7)   51
Leo Dixon (8)   51
Tanesha Flynn (7)   52
Hannah Read (8)   52
Lucy Allan (7)   53
Danielle Booth (8)   53
Yasmine-Rose Bailey (8)   54
Macauley Cormack (7)   54

Amy Gardiner (8)   55
James Wardle (7)   55

Mithian Primary School
Isabel Hunt (9)   56
Iona Sanderson (10)   56
Daniel Rose-Jones (11)   57
Chy Start-Walter (10)   57
Kerra Gibbons (11)   58
Dan Scott (10)   58
Mhairi Purves (11)   59
Oliver Coyle (10)   59
Hannah Whitbread (9)   60
Brittany Snook (9)   60
Zachary Whitbread (7)   61
Wilf Waters (10)   61
Alice Rowling (7)   61
Daisy Kemp (10)   62
Sarah Parry (10)   62
Josh Bierton (9)   63
Michael Bierton (11)   63
Mark Stevens (9)   64
Sam Evans (7)   64
Joshua Job (8)   64
Saskia Maxwell (8)   65
Harry While (9)   65
Holly Callan (8)   66
Harry Waters (9)   66

Mylor Bridge Primary School
Alexandra Taylor (9)   67
Sam Taylor (9)   67
Tom Finney (10)   68
Jenna Bailey (9)   69
Timothy Howe (10)   69
Jowan Rogers (10)   70
Joanna Coles (10)   70
Oliver Barnicoat (9)   71
Jessica Halvorsen (9)   71
Melissa Callaghan (10)   72
Jahrina Barratt (10)   72

Adam Roberts (9)	72
Joel Rose (10)	73
Robert Hooper (10)	73
Chloe Hocking (10)	74
Oliver Katz (9)	74
Melanie Burley (10)	74
Rebecca Rowe (10)	75
Jack Mooney (9)	75
Peter Czunys (9)	76
James Roberts (9)	76
George Vinnicombe (10)	76
Katie Fenton (9)	77
Keiran Taylor (9)	77
Harry Evans (9)	78
Lauren Jose (10)	78
Lucy Shermon (9)	79

Otterton Primary School

Naomi Clarke (8)	79
Freddie Jones (8)	80
Saski Farrington (7)	80
Pippa Glanville (8)	81
Samuel Smith (8)	81
Tom Dufall (7)	82
Hannah Hawkins (8)	82
Emily Keliher (7)	83
Bradley Hayman (7)	83
Sarah Brown (8)	84
Hayden McDonald (8)	84
Callum Archibald (7)	85
Scott Hill (8)	85
Jake Baker	86

Roselands Primary School

Rebecca Lawrence (11)	86
Siân Lenthall (10)	87
Lauren Dawkins (9)	87
Ryan Morey (10)	88
Lauren Thomas (8)	88
Conor Morey (7)	89
Cory Stephenson (8)	89

Tarah Courtenay (9)	89
Sam Frost (10)	90
Craig Barton (9)	91
Jade Marie Coram (10)	91
Samuel Parker (9)	92
Michael Anning (8)	92
Claire Brooking (9)	93
Krystina Murray (9)	93
Stewart Darke (11)	94
Chloè-Sharn Dorrell (11)	94
Ivan Strul (11)	94
Marcus O'Hara (10)	95
Campbell Dougherty (8)	95
Chloe Gibbons (9)	96
Amber Hodgson (9)	96
Callan Fadian (7)	97
Paige Elford (8)	97

St Mary's CE Primary School, Truro

Natalie Crockford (10)	98
Emma Bolt (10)	98
Sophie Evans (10)	99
Amanda Louise Richards (10)	99
Kate Ashton (10)	100
Kensa Knuckey (10)	100
Tegan Endean (10)	100
Bethany Willson (10)	101
Bria Fay (10)	101
Kara Boothby (10)	102
Daniel Peter Ballett (10)	102
Emma Unwin (9)	103
Laura Ann Thomas (10)	103
Sian Williams (10)	104
Aarron Ingleby-Oddy (10)	104
Harry-James Henley (9)	104
Richard Mercer (9)	105
Samantha Tregunna (9)	105
Alexander Caddy (10)	106

St Mewan CP School, St Austell

Chelsea Letcher (8)	106
Daniel Jordan Berry (9)	107
Charlotte Cutlan (8)	107
Ashleigh Hellier (8)	108
Georgia Parkin-Jones (7)	108
Tom Westlake (9)	109
Hayley Watts (8)	109
Luke Perkes (8)	110
Bethany Martin (8)	110
Deanna Paull (8)	111
Zachary Vaughan (8)	111
Alex Perkes (8)	112
Lucy Lund (8)	113
Grace Nichole Digweed (9)	114
Hannah Kendall (9)	115
Charlotte Ann Kiddy (9)	116
Sarah Roberts (9)	117
Charlie Andrew French (8)	118
Matthew Wellington (8)	119
Adam Allerton (9)	120
Amy D Sweet (9)	121
Tessa Marie Isted (8)	122
Lucy Rothero (9)	123
Victoria Cocks (9)	124
Jenna Trudgeon (9)	125
Samuel Joseph Moore (9)	126
Rachel Nottle (8)	127
Thomas Snell (8)	128
Elliot James Baker (8)	129
Alicia Smerdon (9)	130
Christopher Allen (9)	131

St Peter's CE Junior School, Tavistock

Tamsin Pritchard (8)	131
Daryl Panter (9)	132
Emma Champion (8)	132
Luke McClung (8)	133
Bethany Horton (7)	133
Katie Bolt (8)	134
Georgia Mary Bartlett (8)	134

Daniel Allan (8)	135
Jacob Rose (9)	135
Matthew Woodhouse (8)	136
Timothy Davidson (8)	136
Laura Hooper (9)	137
Josh Hosking (8)	138
Samuel O'Boyle (8)	138
Francesca Lois White (7)	139

Salisbury Road Junior School

Ryan Foster (11)	139
Andrew Clarke (10)	139
John Hawkins (11)	140

Tregadillett Community Primary School

Josh Hall (10)	140
Ashton Oak (10)	141
Siobhan Nelson (11)	141
Gemma Crook (11)	142
Ruby Griffiths (10)	142
Shane Sandercock (10)	143
Christopher Allen (11)	143
Nikki Pannell (11)	144
Lucy Griffiths (11)	144
Patsy Griffiths (11)	145
Emma Hancock (10)	145
Daniel Petersen (10)	146
Dale Wallington (9)	147
Sam Mercer (10)	148
Alexander Cornish (10)	148
Laura Dymond (11)	149
Rebekka Wadland (11)	149
Rebecca Pethers (11)	150
Melissa Marshall (11)	150

Victoria Road Primary School

Jordan Sheridan (10)	151
Stacey Buckingham (11)	151
Leah Bailey (11)	152
Natasha Bennett (11)	152
Dwaine Blaby (10)	153

Shaun Brotherston (10)	153
Jamie Cook (10)	153
William Edney (9)	154
Carl Hollyhead (11)	154
Kierun Tungate (11)	155
Ashton Churchill (11)	155
Antony Tungate (10)	156
Ryan Williams (11)	156
George Coulson (10)	157
Samantha McCluskey (11)	157
Luke Barnes (11)	157
Corrie Austin (11)	158
Georgina Wellock (10)	158
Jadie McGinnes (10)	158
Sam Austin (11)	159
Jake Dell (11)	159
Brendan Sturge (10)	159
Jade Victoria Elliott (10)	160
Jasmin Poole (11)	160
Jason Pearson (9)	161
Jasmin Evans-Viney (9)	161
Elisha Brogan (10)	161
Kyle Matthews (10)	162
Joe Oldham (11)	162
Jacob William Eyre (11)	162
James Herbert (10)	163
Chad Johnson (10)	163
Alex J Westmore (11)	164

Yealmpton Primary School
Cushla McDonald (8)	164
Miranda Heath (8)	165
Charlotte Beaumont (8)	165
Daniel Dennis (8)	166
Jack Hooper (8)	166
Scott Magrath (8)	166
Ellie Rogers (9)	167
Charlotte Hendry (8)	167

The Poems

I Stood In A Room

I stood in a room full of thoughts,
My brain booming with allsorts.

I stood in a room full of evil
And walked out the door all feeble.

I stood in a room full of money
And all my senses went funny.

I stood in a room full of the dead
And I found that none of them had a head.

I stood in a room full of giggles,
Where everyone had the wiggles.

I stood in a room full of slime,
Where the church bells never chime.

I stood in a room full of fate,
When I realised it was too late.

I stood in a room which was Heaven,
No longer was I eleven.

Abby Perratt (11)
All Saints CE Primary School

The Owl

The owl swoops and does the loop the loop.
She glides swiftly through the silver night.
Watching her prey throughout the flight.
Her prey stabbed when she grabbed.
Her claws glistening and the night watching and listening.
She flew silently back to the nest
To eat the slithery pest.

Jazmine Colley (10)
All Saints CE Primary School

Sea Cat

Sea cat, playing with the ships like mice,
Clawing at them until they disappear into her depths.
In the night she is dark and grim,
All but the reflection of the silver moon
On her watery, black back.
The dawn has come, a golden sun
Warms her shining, cool waters.
She laps up against the jagged, rough rocks.
Sometimes she is calm and gentle.
Her silky purring fills the air.
Other times she is rough and playful
With claws as sharp as knives.
She splashes over the harbour walls
Sending a soft, salty spray over the top.
Sea cat.
Always there.

Jennifer Watts (10)
All Saints CE Primary School

Cat

Milk-drinker.
Tree-scratcher.
Basket-sleeper
Fur-licker.
Mouse-catcher.
Kitten-cuddler.
Fish-eater.
Ball-player.
Cat-scratcher.
Cat-knapper.
Cat.

Matthew Swain (11)
All Saints CE Primary School

I Stood In A Room

I stood in a room full of chocolate
And started to melt.

I stood in a room full of emptiness
And then turned empty.

I stood in a room full of books
And got really bored.

I stood in a room full of adults
And soon blew up.

I stood in a room full of people
But couldn't find myself.

I stood in a room full of music
And soon became famous.

And . . .

I stood in a room full of money
And became very, very rich.

Adam Harrison (10)
All Saints CE Primary School

A Storm

I can light up the sky with my flashes of light
And lash out my forks at the telegraph poles.

I can shout when I'm angry and can hurt your ears,
I can frighten your pets by growling and grumbling.

I can lash on the rooftops
And flood all the drains.

Katie Brown (10)
All Saints CE Primary School

Barn Owl

Amazing hearing,
Beady eyes watch in the night,
Beige, brown, also buff.
Grabs and slices its mouse prey.
You can't get away from him . . .

Hannah Mellor (11)
All Saints CE Primary School

Turkey

A healthy turkey,
Perching well on the feeder.
Waiting, gobble, yum.

Nicola Bowditch (11)
All Saints CE Primary School

Puppy

Jumping around,
Landing on the ground.

Drinking his milk,
He feels like silk.

Playing with me,
It was meant to be.

He falls asleep
And you don't hear a peep.

He's not grumpy,
That's why I love my puppy.

Hanah Mackenie (10)
All Saints CE Primary School

Cheetah

Prancing prowler,
Grumpy growler.

Deadly hunter,
Lazy grunter.

Speedy racer,
He's quite a pacer.

When he is aggressive,
He is very impressive.

Teeth baring,
Red eyes glaring.

At 60mph,
He has unlimited power.

He lurks around in the night,
Giving most of the animals a fright.

What am I?

Robbie Fellingham (11)
All Saints CE Primary School

A Horse!

Good leaper,
Loud neigher,
Excellent prancer,
Lovely jumper,
Hay eater,
Fast runner,
People carrier,
Fun player,
Nice cuddler,
Real lover.

Chloe Edwards (11)
All Saints CE Primary School

The Owl

The owl swoops and serves across the dusty sky.
His beady eyes look swiftly across the dark, dark night.
He grabs and stabs his only prey.
He watches eagerly for another meal.
He glides and flies across the midnight sky.

Michelle Leary (11)
All Saints CE Primary School

The Owl

Soft, white.
Amazing hearing.

Swift, silent.
Twisting head.

Rusty-gold.
Smooth gliding.

Grabs, stabs.
Kill a mouse.

Swoops, swerves.
Eats the mouse.

Christopher Brown (10)
All Saints CE Primary School

The Barn Owl

I swoop and swerve,
Watching for my prey.
I grab it,
Clutching it in my claws.
I nail it to the ground
But it scurries away.
So I scan the fields for the next victim!

Pollyanna Mowbray (11)
All Saints CE Primary School

The Barn Owl

Silent swooper,
Nocturnal pooper.

Swift glider,
Swervy flyer.

Grabby clutcher,
Stabby toucher.

A scary fearer,
Amazing hearer.

Quick rotater,
A meal for him later.

Mice will he seek,
At the edge of night's peak.

A vole in its beak,
Which had its last squeak.

A barn owl.

Robert Mackenzie (10)
All Saints CE Primary School

Little Dancer

She twirled across the stage floor,
She glided like a swan,
That was then but not anymore.
That's all in her memory now.
She thinks about it often
But shall never be able to do it again.
She still has those satin shoes,
Still pink but faded.
She dreams about it all the time.
She can never be a dancer again.

My mother.

Imogen Wehner (9)
Burrington Primary School

Haiku

Up in the attic
A mouse scampers up and down
Like a rumbling train.

In the icy sea
A stunning mink whale splashes
Like a chiming clock.

Jessica Bayes (11)
Chaddlewood Junior School

Haiku

In South Africa
The elegant elephant
As strong as an ox.

In a tough, old shoe
Lay a newborn field mouse
As weak as an ant.

Christopher Ackland (10)
Chaddlewood Junior School

Haikus

On the grassy hills
A baby lamb snuggles up
As a woolly coat.

Down in the ocean
All krill will swim side by side
Like a flock of birds.

Bryony Sue Howell (10)
Chaddlewood Junior School

Animal Haiku

Hiding under trees
Slithers a cold-blooded snake
As slow as a snail.

Deep beneath the sea
A shark hunts for his dinner
Faster than the wind.

Holly Tamlin (11)
Chaddlewood Junior School

Exotic Animals

In woods near a tree
Lives the bulky armadillos
Like moving boulders.

In the rainforest
Orang-utans sit on trees
Like a jungle king.

Sebastian Weavers (11)
Chaddlewood Junior School

Haiku

In the deep, blue sea
Dolphins come and play with me
As happy as a lark.

In the woodland space
Slyly creeps the active fox
As busy as ants.

Emma Gillings (11)
Chaddlewood Junior School

The Sixth Sense: School Joy

The blossoming scent of bluebells
swaying in the calm and gentle breeze.
The colossal-sized trees as they reach towards the sky
to help give us oxygen.
The cold, hard, wooden bench as I lie flat on my back
waiting for something to happen.
The gentle breeze as it rushes through my hair
and past my fingertips.
The soothing rhythm of a flute as the player practices the song
'We All Live In A Yellow Submarine'.
The infants playing happily in the sun
as the older children play rounders in the field nearby.
The rough and bumpy tree bark as I sit down
underneath its cool shade.
The silver polish as I gaze at the team trophy.
The clock as its hands move second by second
as its time passes by.

Tim Harrison (11)
Chaddlewood Junior School

Animal Nature

On the hot desert
It slithers on ground slowly
As strong as an ox.

In the forest green
It moves as fast as can be
As fast as a hare.

In the dark forest
Moves a dark creature so fast
As sly as a fox.

In the dirty mud
Fat, greedy pigs roll around
Like a silly sheep.

Jodie Downie (11)
Chaddlewood Junior School

Super Summer Senses From School

A past-away plane humming out of sight
into the forever-building clouds.

The flavour of the food
drifting down the so-long corridor.

The birds singing down to us cheerfully
with their feathers puffed up.

The bulky bench's blisters
are smoother than pebbles.

The fluttering and flapping of small wings
outside in the mighty trees.

The damp willow leaves brushing against my head
making me wet.

The entwined roots
rocketing out of the moist ground.

A grass trimmer in the distance
buzzing like a horde of bees stinging someone.

The trees swaying silently
in the whipping wind.

The ear-piercing screech of a whistle
down in the field.

Miles Tarrant (11)
Chaddlewood Junior School

Haikus

In a dense woodland
A dancing blue tit searches
Like a flitting fly.

In the big jungle
A mighty lion does prowl
Like a secret spy.

Sarah Bunney (10)
Chaddlewood Junior School

My Senses Coming To Life

Distant traffic zooming past me.
An aeroplane slowly flying across our school.
Birds singing note by note joyfully.
The pens of other people gently swifting their thoughts on
the page.
The cough of someone working hard, trying not to disturb anyone.
Someone in the distance playing the piano softly.
Children stomping and running around in a rush.
The screams of youngsters arguing over nothing.

The fresh air skimming my tongue.
The smell of freshly-cut grass jumping on my taste buds.
Food cooking in the kitchen while I'm dying of hunger.
Coffee drifting down the corridor from the staff room.

A daydreamer slowly drifting into another world.
The hardworking faces of my classmates, puzzled
and concentrated.
A lonely bag hovering away in the wind, making me feel sorry
for it.
A bluebell all alone weeping and dying because of the lack
of water.
Books calling my name, 'Katherine, Katherine,' desperate for me
to read them.

Katherine Harris (11)
Chaddlewood Junior School

Animal Haiku

In the deep, blue sea,
Gracefully swims a dolphin,
Like a great gymnast.

In Antarctica,
Plods the lazy Polar bear,
Like a very old cat.

Kirsty Kellett (11)
Chaddlewood Junior School

The Beautiful And Wonderful Senses
Of Chaddlewood Junior!

I see
The bright colours all over our classroom, which fills me with joy.
The reflection of the burgundy curtains on the opposite wall.
I fear the blue steel waiting for me to climb all over it.
The ants and spiders crawling up the tree trunk.
The dappled shadows of everyone around, working hard,
                                              looking around.

I feel
My head as I come across a hard problem in Mental Maths.
The fly crawling up my finger as if it's getting ready to take off like
                                              a plane.
Every so often I feel the cold breeze of air, so nobody gets hot.

I hear
Aeroplanes come rushing furiously from the other side of
                                              the world.
Sounds coming down the corridor from the TV room.
Crunchy, crumbling, crackling, as twigs break into small twigs.
Silence being spoilt by little people playing mummies
                                              and daddies.
Fidgeting of everyone trying to get comfortable as we are in a
                                              small place.
A phone ring as Mr Gribble fakes a phone call and pretends to
                                              talk on the phone.

Gemma Harder (10)
Chaddlewood Junior School

Animal Haiku

In the deep jungle
Prowling watchtower lion
As hungry as wolves

As wise as an owl
A slithering dry, hot snake
Brave as a lion.

Ciaran Headridge (11)
Chaddlewood Junior School

Haiku

In the dark jungle,
A fierce T-rex thuds around,
As strong as an ox.

In the deep, blue sea,
A shark hunts around,
Like a watching hawk.

Nathan Kendall (11)
Chaddlewood Junior School

Haiku

Across the desert
Undulates an angry snake
As fast as lightning.

Along the hilltop
Plods an elderly badger
As slow as a slug.

Emily Roberts (10)
Chaddlewood Junior School

Haiku

High in the blue sky
An eagle hovers slowly
Like a gentle lamb.

In the deep, dark woods
A sly fox hunts down its prey
Like a hungry bear.

Amber Semaine (11)
Chaddlewood Junior School

Nature Is Watching Us

Thunder from the aeroplane gliding through the air.
The fresh air going into my dark mouth when I breathe.
A table with a smooth, shiny surface like clean windows.
Books with a thousand words waiting to be read.
The grass which has only just been cut.

Mr Gribble's footsteps banging wherever he goes
Like an elephant tramping in a rainforest.
The fresh flowers bundling up my nose.
The smooth, silky curtains waiting for the day to turn into night.
The anxious look on the year 4's faces wondering what we
are doing.
The mats are like they have just been trampled on my
cheesy feet.

The chirp, chirp of the bird singing happily.
Sarah R muttering to me and others.
All of my classmates climbing on the trees like monkeys in
a forest.

The cold breeze going past me.
Pre-school shouting at one another.

Bianca-Le Borlace-Trevor (11)
Chaddlewood Junior School

Haiku

Up in the tall tree
Hangs an old, decrepit net
Like a huge monkey.

Walking along ice
Is a huge, wet, Polar bear
As white as snowdrops.

Matthew James Harrison (11)
Chaddlewood Junior School

Haiku

In the cold river
Swims an otter darting round
Like a fast greyhound.

In the busy town
Prowls a hungry fox, pad, pad
Like a starving cat.

In the dark, dark night
A bat flies and hangs around
Like an eagle sleeping.

Deep down in the earth
Slithers a long, twisting worm
Like a bendy twig.

Louise Edwards (11)
Chaddlewood Junior School

Happy Haikus

Down by the lakeside
Elegantly the swan swims
Happy as a lark.

Flapping in the sun
The parrot displays colours
As proud as peacocks.

Falling from the sky
The rose-coloured blossom floats
As light as feathers.

Michelle Goddard (11)
Chaddlewood Junior School

Senses Of The School!

The thunder of an aeroplane furiously flying through the air.
1000 pictures, each telling their own story.
The doors opening to unlock another world.
The footsteps of time passing the days onwards.
The glazed eyes on many people looking and searching.
The hard, smooth surface of the cold, see-through glass.
The smooth, slippery surface of the huge, brown, wooden bench.
The droopy willow branches hanging over me.
The crunching of leaves as I walk through the deep trench.
The hard, rubbly surface of the log as I sit on it.
The desperate cries of an innocent child.
The lapping and splashing of frogs in the pond.
The flute rapidly making noise as it turns it into sweet,
                                                    solemn music.
The rough surface of the bumpy, green carpet.

Michael Hapgood (11)
Chaddlewood Junior School

Haiku

Hidden in shadows
The weasel steals loads more food
As sly as a fox.

Lord of the sewers
An evil-eyed rat at work.
The disease spreader.

Alan Dickins (11)
Chaddlewood Junior School

Go And Open The Box

Open the box.
What's inside?
Let me see.

Is it medals?
Is it secrets?
Go and
Open the box.
Is it
Memories?
Is it
Love?

Go and open the box.
Please.
Open it for me.

If you do I'll send
It away into
The diamond ocean.

Liberty Strang (8)
Cockington Primary School

Summer

Summer is when
Children play happily.
Summer is the sun boiling and
Beaming down on the Earth.

Summer is
The holiday
Season when planes
Fly in the sky.

Summer will always sadly
Come to an end.

Bradley Bowman (9)
Cockington Primary School

Go And Open The Door

Go and open the door,
Maybe the sun is glistening down at the flowers
Like a flowing river.

Go and open the door,
Maybe the precious touch of my dad
Stroking me to sleep.

Go and open the door,
Maybe the wind is blowing past me.

Go and open the door,
Maybe the darkness is shooting by me.

Jessica Stuckey (9)
Cockington Primary School

Go And Open The Door

Go and open the door
Maybe there's a ginger cat
Leaping across the sparkly field.

Go and open the door
Maybe the sun is
Shining upon my house.

Go and open the door
Maybe my family is
Waiting for me splashing in
The shimmering river.

Go and open the door
Maybe a pack of beautiful
Animals are standing there for me.

Kerrie McLean (9)
Cockington Primary School

The Sun

The sun like a Jaffa Cake without the chocolate.
The sun like a big, orange freckle.
The sun like the inside of a pineapple.
The sun like the yellow pollen inside a flower.

Brogan Sargerson (9)
Cockington Primary School

The Moon And Sun

The moon and sun
Are as round as a ping-pong ball
Sitting in the sky.

The sun is hot as raging fire
Spreading along the planet.

The moon is cold as a piece of metal
Buried in snow.

Ellie Glasper (9)
Cockington Primary School

The Firework

A firework like a planet popping in the sky.
A firework like a bottle that has smashed.
A firework like some fairy lights in a dark room.

Harriet Faiers (8)
Cockington Primary School

Summertime

Reflecting, glossy sea
Sandy, golden beach
Leaping, glistening dolphins
The melting sun closed up behind the clouds
Blue, shining boats
Colourful, playful fish
Clapping, spiky crabs
The sparkling daylight of summer is gone.

Abigail Jackson (9)
Cockington Primary School

Go And Open The Door

Go and open the door
Maybe a magical forest
Is whispering the sounds
Of nature like a piano tinkling.

Go and open the door
Maybe the wind's icy breath is
Covering the world.

Go and open the door
Maybe a river is flowing
Through the calm town.

Go and open the door
Maybe there is love, hope
And joy.

Scott Beattie (9)
Cockington Primary School

Go And Open The Door

Go and open the door
There could be all your friends
Waiting for you
Telling you it's your birthday.

Go and open the door
There could be a jungle
With lots of brown monkeys
And white tigers.

Go and open the door
There could be your mum
Putting arms out
Wanting a cuddle.

Joshua Coleman (9)
Cockington Primary School

Go And Open The Door

Go and open the door
Maybe the moon is glistening in the moonlight.
The fresh air blowing in your face.

Go and open the door
Maybe the cold aroma of
Nature is spinning around you.

Go and open the door
Maybe I'll be alone.

Scott Arthurs (8)
Cockington Primary School

Summer In The Air

Reflecting, glossy sea
Sandy, golden beach
Leaping, glistening dolphins
The melting sun closed up behind the clouds.

Summer is here
Echoing mist on the glossy sand
Love and romance are in the sparkly, shooting stars
Midnight dancing on a shimmery beach.
Summer is here.

Tansi Chadwick (9)
Cockington Primary School

Summer Sea Animals

Dippy, diving dolphins,
Squirty, squishy squid,
Summer sea animals.

Fabulous flying fish,
Creepy, crawly crabs,
Summer sea animals.

Scary, sharp-toothed shark,
Slippery, shiny seals,
Summer sea animals.

Antonia Wall (9)
Cockington Primary School

The Box Of Secrets

(Based on 'Magic Box' by Kit Wright)

In my box I will put
A sprinkle of water,
An early touch of frost,
The last word of a book,
A scorching ball of fire
And a piercing scream of a girl.

In my box I will put
The last crashing wave,
The trust of my friend,
The love of my family,
The courage of my favourite teacher
And the support of my gramps.

In my box I will put
All answers of life,
The first day I could walk,
The first word I spoke,
The faith of my friends
And the voices from Heaven.

In my box I will put
The direction of life,
Grass eating a cow,
Children doing as they are told,
People enjoying life as summer approaches
And the dream of Chelsea winning the premiership.

Me and my box
Have been around the world.
It has been dropped in places,
Meeting new faces
And wherever it is,
I hope it remembers me, forever and ever.

Connor Stone (10)
Darite Primary School

In My Box

(Based on 'Magic Box' by Kit Wright)

I will put in my box
The name of the last thing on Earth,
The sound of an instrument,
A picture of a lost ghost from a book,
The name of my best friend
And the special days of my life.

I will put in my box
The first fallen leaf from the last tree,
A diamond flaring with fire,
The coldest place on Earth,
Each sense of a human
And the memories of my life.

I will put in my box
The land, sea and air,
A magical, golden moon with black spots,
An ostrich egg made of many colours,
The last word ever written
And the people I knew throughout my life.

I will put in my box
The first wish on my birthday,
All the gods on the Earth,
A palace of magical wonders,
The last word spoken
And the last day of my life.

My box is fashioned with diamonds and gems,
The lock is made from a feather,
The handle is a cloud plucked from the sky,
My name is engraved in silver.

I shall carry my box from north to south and east to west
To remember forever.

Carl Serpell (11)
Darite Primary School

My Box

(Based on 'Magic Box' by Kit Wright)

In my box I will put
A golden acorn,
A silver leaf being turned,
A magical world beyond the universe,
A lotus flower opening up,
A sea of dolphins.

In my box I will put
A mermaid,
A pirate's ship,
The last ever written word,
A miaow from a kitten,
A growl from a tiger.

In my box I will put
The faith of my mum,
The courage from my dad,
The trust from my brother,
The kindness from my friend,
The love from my family.

My box is fashioned from
A silver and turquoise wave curling round,
An angel's wings form the hinges
And the lock is made of sticky toffee.

When I open my box
My secrets will be whispered to me,
This box will never be opened,
It will be buried with me.
Until then I will treasure it forever and ever.

Charis Ward (9)
Darite Primary School

Our Magic Box

(Based on 'Magic Box' by Kit Wright)

I will put in my box
A shell from the seaside,
One fifth of my heart,
A moment which came true,
One glittering flame of life
And an ocean from the world.

I will put in my box
A book from a dog,
A child's first birthday,
A celebrity's first smile,
A moment of truth
And some shimmering snowflakes.

I will put in my box
A tiger's first cub,
Buffy's first stake,
Avril's first song,
A bar of mouth-watering chocolate
And an apple core.

I will put in my box
A teacher's scaly legs,
The thorn of a prickly plant,
My dog's first pup,
My kindest, best friend
And my hamster's new, shining shoes.

My box is fashioned from
A sparkling icicle,
A shimmering snowflake,
An angel's first pair of wings,
The side of a glistening crystal
And a fluffy cloud's first life.

Emily Jenkins (10)
Darite Primary School

Our Magic Box

(Based on 'Magic Box' by Kit Wright)

I will put in my box,
A golden apple hanging on a tree,
The last ray of sunlight,
A 13th month and the 367th day of the year,
A baby's first cry
And the sound of a song in the distance.

I will put in my box
A pony's first gallop,
The last daisy from my garden,
A child's first watch,
The cold snow when it glaciates my fingers,
A cat eating a dog
And a fish eating a penguin.

I will put in my box
The last Christmas feast,
The first Easter egg,
A ruler drawing a line using a human,
A radiant bear as black as coal,
My favourite cuddly toy
And the hot beach of Florida.

My box is fashioned from
Silver, shiny diamonds,
The clasp is made from the thick lace of my shoe,
The lid is made from my leftover chewing gum.

I shall keep my box on my bright red shelf,
It shall be kept with all my care.
It shall not be touched for it is my one and only treasure.

Only mine!

Lucy Hillman (9)
Darite Primary School

My Magic Box

(Based on 'Magic Box' by Kit Wright)

I will put in my box
A worm flying an aeroplane,
The last sunset,
A man who never dies,
An everlasting nightmare,
The first breath of air
And the world's last source of food.

I will put in my box
A dog that puts a lead on a human,
A thousand wishes,
The world's biggest diamond
Ice so hot it could melt the sun,
A ladder so high it's impossible to climb
And a chair so comfortable.

I will put in my box
My first and last birthday,
A ruler that breaks at first touch,
A shoe made from glass,
The first scream,
The last dream
And a vampire-eating pie.

My box is fashioned with
The finest diamonds.
It has ice cubes for buckles
And a clasp made from a human brain.

I will fly my box
To the hottest and coldest places,
Then, I will bury my box
So my memories will be lost
And never discovered.

Daniel Bolitho (10)
Darite Primary School

My Magic Box

(Based on 'Magic Box' by Kit Wright)

I will put in my box
A mouldy alien on a motorbike,
A hooded gangster in a UFO,
A werewolf in a cobwebbed coffin,
A vampire under the silver moon
And a never-ending nightmare.

I will put in my box
My best Christmas ever,
The last minute of laughter,
A phoenix with shimmering, gold feathers,
The first word from the dictionary
And the 10th commandment.

I will put in my box
The last minute of sunlight,
The dispersal of a seed,
The first planet in the solar system
And a dinosaur.

I will put in my box
Dick King Smith's last book,
The first rhyming riddle
And the cat and his fiddle.

I will put in my box
The peak of Mount Everest,
The last dodo,
The first football match
And a photo of my best friend.

My magic box is fashioned with
Egyptian hieroglyphics,
The hinges are made of shimmering quartz
And the lock is made of an elephant's tusk.

Oliver Jenkins (10)
Darite Primary School

My Magic Box

(Based on 'Magic Box' by Kit Wright)

I will put in my box
The last word of an old man,
The last feather on a bird,
The first word of a dumb man,
The rustle of a leaf,
The sight of a bat.

I will put in my box
The forgiveness of a best friend,
The worries of a mother,
My last thought,
The sky with no sun,
A knight with no armour,
A mouse with no tail.

I will put in my box
A child's first drawing,
A clown that's not funny,
A bird that can't fly,
The last drop of rain,
The best day of my life,
The last words of an animal.

My box is made from
A maiden's snowy wings,
The hinges of my box are made from the Pacific Ocean.
My box will remain in a dark corner
And my secrets will never be known.

Oliver Gunning (9)
Darite Primary School

In My Shoe

(Based on 'Magic Box' by Kit Wright)

I will put in my shoe
A trusty friend who I can rely on,
The last ray of sun,
A baby's first smile,
The end of the rainbow,
Hearing birds tweeting all day long,
The first grey hair on my grandma.

I will put in my shoe
A golden ring,
The last Christmas ever,
A banana eating a monkey,
The smooth sand,
The last thorn on a cactus,
The taste of jelly and ice cream.

I will put in my shoe
Daisies picking humans,
The last man to bounce on the moon,
A golden apple hanging from a tree,
A hot, burning flame,
The brightly-coloured eyes of a human,
A school with no teachers.

This shoe will go through generations of my family,
Hearing the noise of my sister rattling.
It will be sparkly with diamonds
And the laces will be made out of gold.
This shoe I will treasure forever.

Jade Harris (10)
Darite Primary School

Box Of Happiness

(Based on 'Magic Box' by Kit Wright)

I will put in my box
The last day of school,
Love, joy and happiness,
Laughter of a thousand children,
All the sparkling 7 seas
And the end of a beautiful rainbow.

In my box I will put
An ocean full of fish,
A horse as fast as the wind,
A stream as steady as the beating of the drum,
A golden, autumn leaf falling from a tree
And the crying of a wolf.

In my box there will be
The first snowy Christmas,
The seed of every spring flower,
The first time a kitten opens its small, blue eyes,
The sky as green as silky grass,
A frog jumping as high as the sun.

My box will have in it
A sunset on the sandy beach,
My best friend's biggest secret,
The last, soft, red rose petal,
A butterfly with golden wings
And a palm tree with no long palms.

My box is fashioned from
The feathers of an eagle's wings,
The necklace of an Indian,
The scales of a mermaid,
And the colour of every horse's mane.
My box will never be opened, that is, until the world ends.

Emily Dimond (10)
Darite Primary School

Box Of Imagination

(Based on 'Magic Box' by Kit Wright)

In my box there is
A school with no children,
A wave riding a surfboard,
A horse as green as grass,
A mouse eating a cat
And ice as hot as the sun.

In my box there is
A fish eating human and chips,
A snowball as black as coal,
A rock as smooth as silk,
An orange as blue as the sky
And a road driving a car.

In my box there is
A sloth as fast as the wind,
A giraffe as small as an ant,
A house living in a person,
A cow clucking like a chicken
And a duck barking like a dog.

In my box there is
A bug standing on a human,
A tap fixing the plumber,
A book reading a person,
A pinyota hitting a person
And my dad's only black hair.

My box is fashioned from
The fur of a tiger,
Locked by the tusk of a rhino.
There is no key for its opening
As what is inside shall never be seen
Because what is inside is my imagination.

Bridie Hillman (10)
Darite Primary School

My Magic Box

(Based on 'Magic Box' by Kit Wright)

I will put in the box
A pig riding a motorbike,
The only flying dictionary,
A cobra in a washing machine,
A school with no floor,
A non-existing animal
And the hottest flame on Earth.

I will put in the box
The world's greenest apple,
An everlasting tub of butter,
The world's largest spider,
Rubbish that eats the bin,
The last word in a book
And a floppy clock.

I will put in the box
A clock that goes backwards,
A zebra with no stripes
The last teardrop from a minnow,
The clearest diamond from India,
The oldest book made from enamel,
The last person alive.

My box is fashioned with
A sherbet shell,
The hinges are carved from the finest silver,
The clasp is covered in mammoth skin.

I shall fly my box
To the plunging darkness of Mars
And there it will pass time,
It will remain unknown,
However, I will find it . . .

Daniel Norton (10)
Darite Primary School

When I Grow Up

When I grow up
I'm going to go to Mars and back.
I'll live in a house made of chocolate
And catch a falling snowflake on my tongue.
I'll watch a horse riding a cowboy
And a dodo will be my pet.

When I grow up
I'll drive a fluffy white cloud
And I'll never tell a lie.
I'll eat nothing but the finest foods.
My dreams will become reality.
I'll watch a pig fly from my window
And climb to the highest point.

When I grow up
A Polar bear will be my pillow
And foxes will chase hounds.
Brussels sprouts will never be eaten
And I'll see the last ever sunrise.
I'll ride in a kangaroo's pouch
And have all the wisdom of the world.

Now I'm grown up
I haven't done any of these things
And I wish that I hadn't made this list.
But one thing I do wish,
I wish I was young again.

Harry Wallace (11)
Darite Primary School

If Stars Were Fish

They would shoot across the inky-blue sea.
They would glide like a stingray in the salty sea.
They would dance across the shimmering sea.
They would speed in the little stream:
They would hover across the deep, dark pond.

Sophie Gregory (9)
Fremington Community Primary School

The Great Escape

The sun shines as I run,
Over fields of green,
But in the night's dark,
I cannot be seen.

My hind legs help me run,
But tired as I be,
I must keep on going,
Else I'll not be free.

Must be careful as I run,
Not to trip over my ears,
I have to find safety -
And control my fears.

As the eagle approaches,
Faster I run,
But I'm sweating and panting,
From the heat of the sun.

There is nowhere to hide,
That is out of sight,
As the eagle dives,
It gives me a fright.

I can't turn around,
For the fear of its eyes,
And when the night comes,
The stars are his spies.

I need a new saviour,
Someone to save me,
Wait - there in the distance,
What is that I see?

A gap in the Earth -
A rabbit hole,
I must hurry now,
If I'm to get to my goal.

Holly Tibble (10)
Fremington Community Primary School

If Stars Were Fish . . .

If stars were fish . . .
If stars were eels they would spin around in the big ocean.
They would jump in the deep sea.
If stars were golden clownfish they would zoom across the cold,
$$\text{dark sky.}$$
They would hover in the moonlight.
If stars were fish they would be called their normal name
Starfish!

Zoe Everest (9)
Fremington Community Primary School

If Stars Were Fish . . .

They would dart across the rock pools.
They would glide across the moonlit lake.
They would spin through the water like a spinning top.
They would zoom through the deep, blue waters.
They would wriggle through the inky pond.

Esther Seaford (9)
Fremington Community Primary School

If Stars Were Fish . . .

They would dart across the salty sea.
They would float in the back garden pond.
They would zoom in the inky-blue lake.
They would glide in the silver river.
They would speed in the little stream.
They would charge in the enormous ocean.
They would swim around in the glass fish tank.

Melissa Warner (9)
Fremington Community Primary School

If Stars Were Fish

They would glide across the deep, dark ocean.
They would sway in and out of the planets.
They would twirl in and out of the dark, black sky.
As they zoom past the moon
They float across the universe.

Bridget Suzanne Phillips (8)
Fremington Community Primary School

If Stars Were Fish

If stars were fish skimming the icy breeze
Diving through the shimmering water
Looking to each side,
Looking for prey.

If stars were nurse sharks gliding through the galaxy
Looking at Saturn, Mars, sun and stars
Gleaming in the silvery ocean
Then swirling and twirling, nibbling at bits of weed.

Luke Pedlar (9)
Fremington Community Primary School

If Stars Were Fish

If stars were fish they would zoom around the deep, blue sea.
They would spin around like a clownfish.
They would hover around in the deep, blue sea.
They would float around the deep, dark, blue ocean.
They would twirl around like a starfish.
They would float like a seahorse.
They would spin like a shark.

Matthew Newton (9)
Fremington Community Primary School

New School

What if I have no friends?
What if school never ends?
What if I really cry
Because someone gives me the evil eye?

But maybe school's really cool.
What if the kids think I rule?
What if in my work I get an A?
What if I'll be shouting *hooray?*

What if I get kicked hard in the knee?
What if the teachers say I act like I'm three?
What if everyone says I'm a fool
Just because I always drool?

What if we cook and bake?
What if we make a gigantic cake?
What if we have a huge school field?
What if we have drinks that are chilled?

I think school could be fun
But then again it could be glum.

Katherine Stone (10)
Hazeldown Primary School

Frog

Fly licker
Lily pad kicker
Swift swimmer
Water skimmer
Tadpole keeper
Winter sleeper
Slug muncher
Snail shell cruncher
Beetle basher
Insect gnasher.

Emma Roby (11)
Hazeldown Primary School

Seasons

Spring
Scent of fresh flowers
A new beginning for leaves
Birds' first sight of light.

Summer
The smell of chlorine
Sight of red, sunburned people
Odour of sun cream.

Autumn
Chestnuts get eaten
Bonfires fill the air with fireworks
Frost freezes the water.

Winter
Snowmen come again
Christmas is here, presents come out
The tortoise is sleeping.

Matthew Rushton (11)
Hazeldown Primary School

Seasons

Spring sun shining,
A glimmer of new life,
Along with the sea air.

Summer barbecues,
With the tropical sun cream smell,
Swimming in the air.

Autumn leaves rustling,
Trees shedding their dead, brown leaves,
Season's sun's near the end.

Icicles winter,
Crunching footsteps, frozen snow,
Fires lit for warmth.

Hannah Holliday (11)
Hazeldown Primary School

New School

I'm going to TCC,
James and Lloyd
And Chris
And me.

What if the kids bash me black and blue?
What if they flush my head down the loo?
What if they think that they always rule?
What if they chuck me in the swimming pool?

What if the homework is really hard?
What if in football I get a red card?
What if I lose my dinner money?
I wish they would think I was funny.

But on the other hand . . .

What if we get sweets given to us?
What if we get to go on the bus?
What if we cook doughnuts and buns?
What if we get to fight with toy guns?

Big school may not be that bad.
What if the teachers think I'm a good lad?
The big kids may like me and think I'm great.
Lunch, I'll sit with them, dinner on my plate.

Will new school be fun? I don't know!
Will the kids find me friend or foe?

James Treweek (11)
Hazeldown Primary School

There Was An Old Man From Bombay

There was an old man from Bombay
But all he could say was *wey hey.*
He went up to his bed
And banged his big, red head
And that was the man from Bombay.

Emma Lane (10)
Hazeldown Primary School

New School

What if I have no friends?
What if my nightmare never ends?
What if I really cry
Because someone gave me the evil eye?

But what if the school's really cool
And the kids think I rule?
What if we get to cook and bake?
What if I make a chocolate cake?

What if I get a detention?
I'll be late for registration
Then I'll get punched in the face
By a bully with a brace.

Maria Bykova (11)
Hazeldown Primary School

Vicious School Around!

Toilet chatters while the roll bites,
Mirror smashed because of your ugly face.
Pens die because you've wasted their blood,
Pencils get angry and shoot out their lead.
Lights switch and they blink away,
Scissors get out of control and snap at you.
The door slams and laughs with evilness,
The OHP sneezes while it's doing its job.
The clock's heartbeat confuses your mind,
The chairs suck you down to the evil world.
The table's tongue can reach for your neck,
Paper rolls itself up and hits you on the head.

Megan Thomson, Eve Sydenham,
Charlotte L & Maddie W (11)
Hazeldown Primary School

TCC

Will I like TCC?
Will the teachers pick on me?
Will they split me from my friend?
Then the boredom wouldn't end.

What if people bully me?
They could bruise or break my knee.
They could call me names and swear.
That would give me a big scare.

Will the homework be too much?
Will my classroom be a hutch?
Will the teachers think I'm dumb
'Cause I can't do a single sum?

Will I like TCC?
Will the kids adore me?
Great new friends I might make,
Who might give me loads of cake.

Will the new lessons be great?
Little Math might be my fate.
I might cook a big load
And eat until I explode.

Will I like the school dinners?
Will they be prize winners?
Will they be extremely cheap
And the drinks not too weak?

Alice Smiddy (11)
Hazeldown Primary School

10 Things In A Spaceman's Pocket

1. A shooting star too small to be shot.
2. A toothbrush equipped with toothpaste
3. Photos of different people who aren't on Earth.
4. A bit of Mars still in its wrapper.
5. A receipt for the old USA NASA rocket.
6. A tiny alien. There *is* life on Mars.
7. Galaxy wrapper.
8. A laser gun, maybe to fight the aliens.
9. An old book that must have been read 100,000,000 times.
10. Date of birth, 1765.

Jack Kelly Stacey (11)
Hazeldown Primary School

A Teacher's Poem

Mrs Clog has a frog
Sitting on a brown log.

Mrs Pat has a rat
Sleeping on a furry hat.

Mrs Brock has got a one-eyed croc
That gave the postman a mighty shock.

Mr Brat has a cat
Lying on a fluffy mat.

Dr Throat has a hairy goat
Lying on a very furry coat.

Abigail Jopson (8)
Manadon Vale Primary School

Pets Of People

Professor Cowl kept an owl
In a cage under a towel.

Mr Slunk found a skunk
Which he dressed as a punk.

Lord Weep borrowed a sheep,
He read it stories and went to sleep.

Ms Wheel kept a seal
And it made a meal.

Mr Mitt kept a blue tit
Who had a first aid kit.

Hannah French (8)
Manadon Vale Primary School

Croc And Mock

Mrs Mock has a croc
That sits on a block.

Professor Cider has a tiger
That plays with a spider.

Dr Moat has a goat
That has a big, strong throat.

Sir Narot has a parrot
That eats carrots.

Professor Clod has a frog
That stares at fog.

Joshua Edwards (8)
Manadon Vale Primary School

What Do Animals Eat?

Mrs Stoat has a goat
Eating her fuzzy coat.

Professor Hat has a rat
That sleeps under his rigid mat.

Master Harrot hides his carrots
Under his parrot.

Lord Clog found a frog
Then he got a dog to eat the frog.

Sir Fat ate a bat
Then he hit it with a baseball bat.

Scott Hardman (8)
Manadon Vale Primary School

People's Pets

Mrs Brat has a cat
Lying under her furry hat.

Mr Fog has a dog
Hiding inside a big, brown log.

Mrs Lock has a croc
Pretending to be a big, green rock.

Mr Barrot has a stupid parrot
Trying to eat one million carrots.

Professor Moat has a goofy goat
That tries to catch ninety-nine boats.

Samuel Couch (7)
Manadon Vale Primary School

Teachers' Pets

Mrs Clog had a frog
Sitting on a little log.

Mrs Cock had a croc
In her tiny, little sock.

Mr Boat had a goat
On his curious coat.

Professor Stake had a snake
On his shiny, wool cape.

Master Barrot had a parrot
On his trusty carrot.

Miss Tiger had a spider
On her colourful glider.

Miss Mat had a cat
On her red sun hat.

Haaris Khan (8)
Manadon Vale Primary School

Oh No!

Master Glider had a spider
That ate a great big tiger.

Mrs Brock had a one-eyed croc
That gave the postman a mighty shock.

Mr Throat had a goat
Lying on my new coat.

Andrew Pond (8)
Manadon Vale Primary School

Teachers' Pets

Mrs Clog has a little frog
Sitting on a brown log.

Mr Cock has a croc
Swimming in the loch.

Dr Lake has a snake
Making a lovely steak.

Miss Hider has a spider
Drinking lots and lots of cider.

Professor Slider has a tiger
Playing on his toy glider.

Liam Lewis (8)
Manadon Vale Primary School

Teachers' Pets

Mrs Clog has a little frog
Sitting on a brown log.

Mrs Dock has a croc
Lying on her furry frock.

Master Pat has a cat
Sleeping on a big, old mat.

Mr Fake has a snake
Who slithers round a big cake.

Miss Slider has a tiger
Lying on her furry glider.

Amy Gumbrell (8)
Manadon Vale Primary School

Who Pets Live With

Mr Clog had a ragged dog
That ate a giant frog.

Mr Mat had a hairy cat
Eating a big, fat rat.

Mrs Coat had a shaggy goat
Lying on a ferry boat.

Mrs Cock had a rocky croc
Eating a hard, healthy block.

Master Make had a slimy snake
Eating a giant wedding cake.

Kirsten Masters (7)
Manadon Vale Primary School

Where People Keep Pets

Mrs Mog has a 10-foot dog
Lying on a big, fat log.

Mr Mat had a 10-foot cat
Lying on a giant hat.

Mrs Throat has a hairy goat
Lying on a ferry boat.

Mrs Cock had a rocky croc
Eating a hard, heavy block.

Master Cake has a long snake
Eating a chewy steak.

Daniel Jones (8)
Manadon Vale Primary School

Animal Poem

Mrs Chat has a cat
Lying on a mat.

Mr Fat had a cat
With a big, fat rat.

Professor Throat had a goat
With a coat.

Joseph Weinling (8)
Manadon Vale Primary School

The Silly Teachers

Mrs Take had a snake
Lying on a sharp rake.

Mr Hog had a dog
Lying on a hard log.

Mrs Throat had a goat
Lying on a furry coat.

Mrs Vicars had a spider called Stickers
Who ran in her knickers.

Zacharias Evans (7)
Manadon Vale Primary School

Teachers' Pets

Dr Tog had a big, fat dog
Floating along on a log in thick fog.

Lord Barrot had a coloured parrot
Always chewing on a carrot.

Leo Dixon (8)
Manadon Vale Primary School

Teachers' Pets

Mr Gat has one cat
Lying on a thin, small mat.

Mrs Brock has a croc
Sitting by a block.

Master Fogs has 2 dogs
Barking at the little, green frogs.

Dr Barrot has a parrot
Who ate carrot.

Professor Rider has a hairy tiger
Who likes a spider called Sider.

Tanesha Flynn (7)
Manadon Vale Primary School

The Tiger On The Furry Glider

Miss Spider has a tiger
Who plays on her glider.

Mr Hat had a rat
On a furry cat's mat.

Dr Fake made a cake
With a green snake.

Miss Bloc had a croc
On her bestest frock.

Professor Throat had a thin goat
Lying on her white, smooth boat.

Hannah Read (8)
Manadon Vale Primary School

Where Do Animals Live?

Mr Fat had a black cat
Who caught a furry rat.

Mr Block had a wet croc
Inside a big rock.

Father Spider had a tiger
Who went on a slippery glider.

Lady Tiger had a spider
Drinking a glass of cider.

Master Dog had a frog
But it died in a horrid fog.

Lucy Allan (7)
Manadon Vale Primary School

Hairy Dog, Slimy Frog

Mrs Mog bought a dog
Then she bought a slimy frog.

Mr Barrot bought a carrot
For his colourful parrot.

Dr Lake bought a cake
For his slimy snake.

Professor Fat bought a rat
And then he bought a cat.

Master Seal bought an eel
For his lovely meal.

Danielle Booth (8)
Manadon Vale Primary School

People's Pets

Mrs Throat has a furry goat
That bites on her frilly coat.

Dr Glider has a spider
That drinks cider.

Master Mat has a cat
That sleeps on his furry hat.

Mrs Barrot has a parrot
Who eats munchy carrots.

Sir Clog has a frog
Called Mog.

Mr Lish has fish
In a dish.

Miss Mock has a croc
That loves sleeping on a rock.

Yasmine-Rose Bailey (8)
Manadon Vale Primary School

Why Have Pets?

Mrs Fat has a cat
Who lays on a flat mat.

Mrs Stickers lost her knickers
On her way to get a pair of Kickers.

Mr Hider has a spider
Who drinks cider like a glider.

Dr Barrot has a parrot
Who eats his carrot.

Mr Slog has a dog
Who eats a giant frog.

Macauley Cormack (7)
Manadon Vale Primary School

Then I Bought . . .

Mrs Mog bought a dog
Then she bought a slimy frog.

Mr Throat bought a goat
And his bed was a little, white coat.

Mrs Barrot bought a parrot
And he said, 'I want that carrot.'

Master Drake bought a lake
And it looked like a little, blue cake.

Dr Neal bought a seal
And it ran like a little, green eel.

Amy Gardiner (8)
Manadon Vale Primary School

The Animals Of The Wood

Miss Mock has a croc
That sits on a block.

Mrs Throat has a hairy goat
That sits on a hairy coat.

Mr Matt has a cat
That sits on a tiny mat.

Sir Marrot has a parrot
That eats carrots.

Dr Slog has a dog
That eats a big log.

James Wardle (7)
Manadon Vale Primary School

Hibernation

Squirrels scurrying round and round,
Rabbits burrowing without a sound.

Getting ready for winter's cold,
Only the robin stands brave and bold.

The bear also makes her lair,
Making her young get the best of care.

The hedgehog buries himself down deep,
Getting ready for his winter sleep.

In spring when the air is warm,
They will at last wake
Dismantling the nests they took so long to make.

Out go the feathers and warm turf,
In come the grass and flowers and earth.

Isabel Hunt (9)
Mithian Primary School

The Unicorn

Sleek and shiny, black hooves pound
Pattering gently on the ground
Balanced upon the head a pointing horn
His soft mane golden as corn
Tail swishing, batting flies
Under the blossom tree he lies
A flick of the tail, he jumps up high
And flies into the sky
As the colt came to a halt
He saw something far away
And gave a wickering neigh
This is the end of the adventure and the end of the day.

Iona Sanderson (10)
Mithian Primary School

Steam Engines And Tin Mines

Old Smokey a-puffing along
The roller a-squashing the road
In front of it a castle with a moat
In the river nearby a steam boat
Next a steam fair
Lots of steam engines there
Stationary engines turn the rides
Miniature engines puff by the sides.

150 years ago an engine house stands
A-puffing away for the tin
While down in the mine miners a-digging
Awaiting their pay for the day
While up above a steam engine takes the tin away
But that now has stopped, the last mine a-closing
But some steam engines do still run.

The track is a-rumbling
A steam train roaring by
Still going in this day and age.

Let's hope that they never do stop.

Daniel Rose-Jones (11)
Mithian Primary School

The Spider

Crawling along the walls with people standing beneath it,
Getting ready to sting you,
As it digs its fangs into your arm,
Its poisonous venom makes you sleepy.
You get rushed to hospital,
The spider gets left alone.
Say goodbye to your house.

Chy Start-Walter (10)
Mithian Primary School

Why?

Why do the stars only show at night?
Is it so the birds don't bump into them in flight?
Why is the grass always green
And the leaning tower on a lean?
Why do the clouds not fall down on us?
Are they held up with string?
Why is God invisible
And ghosts so unseeable?
Why is war happening every day
So children can't go out and play?
Why are people dying?
Why are people killing?
Why is the world turning into this?
Help it stop
And save the world.

Kerra Gibbons (11)
Mithian Primary School

Pipeline

The offshore wind beats on my face
I pass the white water and the swimmers' race
I paddle out back and watch the fish
And then I see that wave, the hardest dish
I paddle and paddle, I get up on my board
I slice through the water like a steel sword
I go in the tube but only to wipe out
My leash is caught, I fumble about
But I swim up to the top
With my hair like a mop
And swim back to the shore
All aching and sore.

Dan Scott (10)
Mithian Primary School

Colourful Feelings

Through shade upon shade of aquamarine and sapphire,
Set below burnished gold,
Hand upon helpful fin and skin to silky skin,
In joyful oneness with their graceful strength,
I swam with gentle dolphins.

Trudging and staggering, coldly determined,
Through whirling white and glacial glitter;
Across crystal chasms and frozen floes,
Ploughing through shifting drifts of snow upon snow,
I journeyed to the Pole.

As I blasted off to the violet vastness of space,
It came for me, creeping on stealthy feet;
Drawing me back to my shadowed pillow,
A stricken statue of terror,
Shaken by my heart's tumultuous beat.

A sighing drone, a grumbling groan.
A growling voice trying to talk?
A rattling, rumbling drawn-out moan.
Good morning! It's time for my walk.

With a jump and a bump and a slithering slump,
I could feel his hot breath on my head!
Not a ghoul with a curse, not a monster or worse . . .
Just my dog, jumping on my bed!

Mhairi Purves (11)
Mithian Primary School

The Otter

Gliding through the water
Like a knife through butter.
Swift as an arrow flying through the air.
It moves as fast as a cheetah in central sprint.
Now the otter has swum away
As swift as a sword
And it will come back once more.

Oliver Coyle (10)
Mithian Primary School

Winter Wonderland

I'm shuffling my feet in the white, white snow,
I look up at the sky where robins flow,
I gaze at the patch where pansies did grow,
Covered up by the white, white snow.

It's winter,
It's white everywhere,
It's a winter wonderland.

I hear the laughing of children nearby,
I see a snowball fly through the sky,
I soon hear a faint blackbird's cry,
But now it's time to say goodbye.

It's winter,
It's white everywhere,
It's a winter wonderland.

Hannah Whitbread (9)
Mithian Primary School

My Fabulous Dog Edward

My dog is a white Boxer dog.
He lives on a building site.
He barks and barks all day and night.
He can see in the dark with red, gleaming eyes.
When he is hungry he eats cottage pies.
He catches hoops and sticks and is very good at tricks.
He chases the chickens and barks at the cars.
He lazes around and sits on the sand piles
And that's why I say, this very day,
He's mine, he's mine, he's mine.

Mine!

Brittany Snook (9)
Mithian Primary School

My Baby Brother

My baby brother cries a lot
And he also smiles a lot
And at night when I go to sleep
I kiss him on his little cheek.

Zachary Whitbread (7)
Mithian Primary School

The Sea

The sea is like a snarling beast,
Crashing and smashing against the rocks.

Sending sea spray into the sky,
Splashing against children's faces as they're playing.

But in the night the waves so big
Come crashing down turning rocks to pebbles.

But in the morning it all calms down,
Allowing people to surf and children to play.

Wilf Waters (10)
Mithian Primary School

I Am Sure I Saw A Bee Go By . . .

I am sure I saw a bee go by
Yellow and black, up to the sky
His busy wings
His sharp stinger
He sounds like a great singer.

Alice Rowling (7)
Mithian Primary School

The Prince Philip Races

The brakes squeaked as the lorry ground to a halt,
Inside the car my heart did somersaults.

It was the day of the Prince Philip Games,
Which were held in Bristol, down long, muddy lanes.

First it was time for the best-turned-out,
The judges were strict, there was no doubt.

Next it was time for the races,
Which put pony and rider through their paces.

Then we went home with a rosette,
It had been a day to never forget.

Daisy Kemp (10)
Mithian Primary School

The Mermaid

The mermaid's tail sparkles in the sun.
In a purple, green and blue lagoon,
She sings to the seals and the moon.
Her voice is so beautiful the waves go calm.
In the day she sits on a rock,
By a deserted beach.
She sings and combs her long, golden hair.
She jumps off the rock and falls into the sea,
Ever so elegantly
And is gone.
All you can see now
Is a flicker of purple, blue and green.
The flick of a tail up in the air.

Sarah Parry (10)
Mithian Primary School

The Day I Had A Squirrel

The day I had a squirrel,
It was on a Monday.
It wasn't on a Friday
And it wasn't on a Sunday.
It gnawed through all the curtains,
It gnawed through all the stairs,
It gnawed through all the tables
And it gnawed through all the chairs!

The day I had a squirrel,
It was on a Monday.
It wasn't on a Friday
And it wasn't on a Sunday.
It terrified my hamster,
It terrified my cat,
It terrified my gerbil
And it terrified my rat!

Josh Bierton (9)
Mithian Primary School

Watch The Birdie

Sitting, still as a stone,
With a pair of binoculars at my side,
I watch the robin peck the seeds
That I threw out from where I hide.

From under the table I notice
A cat creeping up on the bird.
The cat leaps out - and misses
And fluttering away is the bird.

Michael Bierton (11)
Mithian Primary School

Steam

Old Smoky puffing down the road
Little Smoky shunting
A fairground load
The old Mamod steamroller
Moving up the road
Pulling a very big load
The putt-putt boats chuffing by
Never again in a wink of an eye
Shining engines choking by.

Mark Stevens (9)
Mithian Primary School

Dogs

Big, small, short, tall.
Fat, slim, clever, dim.
All you have to do
Is to choose one to suit you!

Sam Evans (7)
Mithian Primary School

The Rough Sea

The sailors bring their boats in
The lights are on
The foghorn goes off
The spray comes up from the harbour wall
The seal is struggling
It paddles to the shore
The sea is calming down
The seal goes back and swims away
All the mist has gone for today.

Joshua Job (8)
Mithian Primary School

My Dog Sam

My dog Sam is a silly, old dog
He always sleeps just like a log.
He plays around all the day,
Chasing pheasants
And sneaking away.
He jumps around
And I throw him sticks.
My dog Sam is a silly, old man.
Even though he is so funny
I just love him as he is my Sam.

Saskia Maxwell (8)
Mithian Primary School

The Cat I Chased One Day

The cat I chased one day
Was chasing a piece of hay.
The cat I chased one day
Was rolling a bit of clay
And by the time it finished
It looked like a rat.

The cat I chased one day
Was chasing a rat,
Rolling in a hat,
Down a hill.
By the time it got to the bottom
The cat was tied in cotton.

Harry While (9)
Mithian Primary School

My Rabbit Parsley

My rabbit Parsley is very funny,
Not just because he is a bunny.
He likes to sit in a plant pot
Even when it's really hot.

When my friend came to play
It was a very sunny day.
Parsley charged to the gate
But he was too slow, he was too late.

And now he stays safe with me,
He always likes to have his tea.
With pointy ears and jumpy feet,
He loves to lick and he loves to greet.

Holly Callan (8)
Mithian Primary School

Harvest Time

As I am walking by the fields
Pumpkins and sweetcorn are now revealed,
Golden hay bales are stacked so high
They may even touch the sky,
Rose-red leaves floating gently down
Hundreds of them cover the ground,
The farmers gather the crops
And put them into shops,
Vegetables and fruit are in their prime
Because now it's joyful Harvest Time!

Harry Waters (9)
Mithian Primary School

Sea Sounds

The sea is a lion
Roaring, crashing,
Smash, smash, smash,
Smash against the rocks.
Splash on the shore,
Spray flicking the air,
Seagulls swooping and screeching,
Wind whistling through the caves.

But when it's calm,
It's as quiet as a mouse,
No splashing, no crashing,
No roaring, quiet peace.
Just peace, peace.
Just water creeping peacefully
Along the silent, sandy shore.

Alexandra Taylor (9)
Mylor Bridge Primary School

Icy Streets

I am inside, looking outside,
At people walking and slipping,
As if they are ice-skating,
In the freezing cold street.
They shiver and shake,
Like a telephone ringing,
As they slither on their feet,
In the icy cold,
As if they were old.

Sam Taylor (9)
Mylor Bridge Primary School

Greedy Growler

My dog,
Is a bit of a hog.
All day eating non-stop,
And always stealing from the local shop.

As you can imagine he's very fat,
Far too big to sit on his mat.
He scoffs sausages, steak and Bonios,
He's even too fat to scratch his nose.

One day when digging a hole,
He hit something hard and found a mole.
He fell in,
With a terrible din!

He couldn't get out,
So gave a shout!
Nobody heard,
Except a passing bird.

The bird flew down,
To the ground,
To tell the dog's master,
About the disaster.

The master came,
The dog was in shame.
He tugged the dog,
But he was as stuck as a log!

The master went *um* and *ar*,
And drove off in his car.
He came back with a large steak,
And a delicious cream cake.

He waved the goodies in front of the dog,
Who leapt out of the hole like a frog!
So the moral of the story . . .
Don't eat too much or things will get gory!

Tom Finney (10)
Mylor Bridge Primary School

I Love Snow!

I am inside, staring outside,
At the snowmen big and bold,
The dainty snow fairies,
Darting around in winter's cold.

I am outside, staring inside,
At the glowing coal fire,
The colours bright, glowing red,
They're just so nice to admire.

I am inside, looking outside,
At the whirling, twirling snow,
The ash burning in the fire,
With a red and yellow glow.
It makes me shiver,
For it's bitter and cold
Out there, but in here,
I am as warm as the cat I hold.

Jenna Bailey (9)
Mylor Bridge Primary School

Squirrels

Squirrels like scurrying,
Through the trees.
They're always hurrying,
Collecting leaves.
They never have time to stop,
They run along like a piston on a train.
They eat their nuts until they pop,
They store the nuts when the weather is rain.
They fly down the trees with the greatest of ease,
And sail up again with the help of the air.
Up and down like swarming bees,
They live in the trees without a care.

Timothy Howe (10)
Mylor Bridge Primary School

My Bike Ride!

Here I go on my bike,
Gravel sliding, what a sight.
Mud splashing,
Adrenalin pumping,
Pedals in flight.

Down by the river as I ride by,
Startled ducks and woodcocks fly,
Sailboats sailing, children, playing,
Water lapping on the rocks,
Look at my watch. Now I can't stop!

Homeward bound as my wheels go around,
Winds whistling through my hair,
Legs aching, gears racing,
Up the hill we go
Home again, safe and sound,
With my two feet back on the ground.

Jowan Rogers (10)
Mylor Bridge Primary School

In The Playground

Children shouting and screaming,
Boys playing and running,
Girls gossiping in corners,
Leaves falling and twirling,
Whilst the classrooms are still and quiet,
Balls flying out of nowhere,
Presumably they've been kicked,
Bells ringing for assembly,
That's the end of our playground visit.

Joanna Coles (10)
Mylor Bridge Primary School

Fireworks

At night is when the fireworks come
Crashing, swooshing, booming, lots of fun
They light the sky, nice and bright
The turbo jet rockets bang, giving you a fright.

The children hold sparklers in their hands
While the fireworks are soaring over the land
Blue, purple, yellow, orange and green
It is the greatest sight I have ever seen.

Children standing with Mum and Dad
In the home dogs barking, going mad
In the garden it was rainy and cold
But I couldn't miss the colours, exciting and bold.

Me and my friends standing there
Watching the colours in the air
When the fireworks and sparklers are out
'Same time, next year,' we all shout!

Oliver Barnicoat (9)
Mylor Bridge Primary School

The Dolphin

Dolphins diving here and there,
Over waves without a care,
Lazily gliding through the sea,
Perfect animals so gentle and free,
Happily they talk and play,
In the water they frolic all day,
Naturally beautiful and smart,
Surely a wonderful work of art!

Jessica Halvorsen (9)
Mylor Bridge Primary School

The Cat

It sneaks like a tiger around the house,
Getting ready to pounce on its prey
And when you go into the garden,
You'd better watch out
Because it might be coming for you today.

Melissa Callaghan (10)
Mylor Bridge Primary School

Thunder And Lightning

Crash, bang!
Bang, flash!
Flash, flash!
Rumble, boom!
Rumble, lots of little lights.
Rumble, big bangs booming.
Crash, bad for barbecue!
Crash, smash!
In with a dash!
Barbecue night is inside now.
It was fun, but now it's done.

Jahrina Barratt (10)
Mylor Bridge Primary School

The Beach

Waves crashing on the beach like thunder.
The waves sucking the pebbles like a Hoover, back into the sea.
Seagull swooping like a glider.
Each rock pool is an individual village.
Crabs playing hide and seek in the seaweed forest.
Sand like golden sugar surrounds rocks, like small mountains.

Adam Roberts (9)
Mylor Bridge Primary School

The Four Seasons

Spring comes, ends rainfall,
Buds start to spread all around,
It is getting warm.

Summer brings out heat,
Bees are busy in the sun,
Families have fun.

Autumn comes, leaves brown,
Squirrels gather some more food,
The park is deserted.

Winter comes, snow falls,
Families open presents.
Animals sleeping.

Joel Rose (10)
Mylor Bridge Primary School

Thunder At Night

Crash!
Crumple,
Crumble,
Caboosh!
Slosh,
Crackle,
5, 4, 3, 2, 1,
Bing,
Bang,
Creak,
Boom!
The storm steals away,
The thunder goes shy with fear,
The lightning got quieter and quieter.
This is the end of the storm.

Robert Hooper (10)
Mylor Bridge Primary School

Out In The Woods

Out in the woods,
Out in the woods.
A buzzard sleeps,
A wolf-pack howls.
The trees weep,
A lost cat miaows.
Out in the woods,
Out in the woods.
Some animals sleep
As if they're dead.

Chloe Hocking (10)
Mylor Bridge Primary School

Seaside Sounds

Swish, crash as the sea breaks,
Tooooo as the sea smashes onto the cliff,
Eeack, eeack, seagulls screech over people low,
Splosh as the ice cream falls onto the cone,
Whoo, whooo as the windmills whirl round,
Boom, smash as the sea breaks again.

Oliver Katz (9)
Mylor Bridge Primary School

Percking Pancakes

Sizzle, sizzle, splish, splat,
Flop, flip up in the air!
Bubble, spit, hear the bubbles whoosh,
Crackle, crackle, the butter's melting.
Flip, flop, flip, flip,
Munch, munch,
Sunday's dinner's gone!

Melanie Burley (10)
Mylor Bridge Primary School

City Noises

In the city lights flash,
And cars crash!
Motorbikes whiz,
As quick as a flash,
People quickly dash.

Horns beeping all the time,
Beep, beep, beep, beep
Just like a rhyme,
Buses starting,
Brummmmm-brumming,
The world is humming.

Rebecca Rowe (10)
Mylor Bridge Primary School

Football Match

Football match,
Balls clatter against feet,
People shouting,
Whistles blowing,
Wind whistling,
Horns beeping.
When someone scores,
The crowd goes wild,
Like a hungry tiger roaring.
The final whistle blows,
The crowd cheer,
Players clap each other,
Everyone chatters as they leave the ground,
Then all is peaceful.

Jack Mooney (9)
Mylor Bridge Primary School

The Sea

Caves dripping,
Waves splashing onto rocks,
People shouting,
Screeching seagulls lurking.
People rushing to their cars,
Engines running,
Pebbles scratching.
Beach empty,
Tide rolling in.

Peter Czunys (9)
Mylor Bridge Primary School

Parisian Pigs

Pigs in Paris
Pull practical jokes on poodles,
Perform plays for penguins,
Pinch pets and petrol,
Pass plagues to puffins and parrots,
Party with presidents and police,
While panthers play pinball,
Pandas petrify pygmies in pantaloons.

James Roberts (9)
Mylor Bridge Primary School

Summer

Summer, summer, lots of sun.
Summer, summer, always fun.
Summer, summer, apple dunking.
Summer, summer, ice melting.
Summer, summer, hot days.
Summer, summer, always.
Summer, summer, really cool,
Summer, summer, jumping into the pool.

George Vinnicombe (10)
Mylor Bridge Primary School

My Temptation

I am always tempted to steal sweets from the top of the fridge,
But I hardly ever get to it from the creak of the hinge.
My mum always hears, when eeek,
There comes an enormous creak.
I've only managed it once, when I was little,
When the sound was drowned by the whistling kettle.
One, two, three, four, five, six, seven, eight, yes eight,
But then I heard the calling, 'Kate,
Kate, Kate, what have you done?
You know that it isn't much fun,
When you take all the sweets you see
And don't leave any for Jess and me!'

Katie Fenton (9)
Mylor Bridge Primary School

Keiran's Pets

In his bedroom Keiran kept:
10 monkeys that battered bananas
9 kangaroos that hop and jump
8 budgies that go cheep
7 snakes that slither
6 lions that pounce
5 rabbits that bounce
4 fish that swim around
3 tortoises that plod along
2 spiders that weave their webs
and 1 . . . guess what?

Keiran Taylor (9)
Mylor Bridge Primary School

Wintertime

I am inside, staring outside,
At the bright, white, falling snow.
Every house covered with a dust of icing sugar,
Trees like white, rubber gloves.
People zooming on a sledge like a rocket,
Going into outer space.
Fields like a blanket of white wool.
I am outside glaring inside,
At the blazing, colourful fire.
Children drinking warm, hot chocolate,
As they doze next to the fire,
Glowing, because they've played in the snow.

Harry Evans (9)
Mylor Bridge Primary School

View From A Window

Peering out of the window,
At the whirling waves creeping up the beach,
The dogs scampering in the dunes,
Beyond their reach.
The high, rugged cliffs,
Watching, waiting,
Like the giants of ancient myths.
On the horizon, houses in a row,
That's what I see out of my dad's window.

Lauren Jose (10)
Mylor Bridge Primary School

Snow

I am inside, looking outside
At the fluttering snow
Which turns and twirls
Like feathers floating in the air
Making the cold, wet ground
Look like icing sugar on a cake.
Whilst I am inside in the warmth
With the red and yellow, flashing flames
Of the fire flickering in the shadows
But I can't wait to run outside
Into white, feathery snow.

Lucy Shermon (9)
Mylor Bridge Primary School

Dotty, Little Lion Cub

I'm an idling, little lion cub,
You can hardly see me because I'll hide behind a shrub.
It's hard to catch me (I'm quick on my feet)
Or as the French might say, 'Veet, veet, veet!'
I'm the opposite to my brother Joe and my sister Heather
(Because you must know they're not very clever!)

My daddy is the king of the jungle,
But he's not really all that humble.
I love to eat lollipops,
My mum has to buy them from sweet shops.
When I get hot and bothered and not in a good mood,
I can be very, very rude.

Naomi Clarke (8)
Otterton Primary School

Silly Shark

I'm a silly shark,
I'm friends with a lark,
I lost a fin, found it in the bin
Then I drank a bottle of gin!

I'm called Woopy,
I'm friends with Goopy,
I normally go loopy
And I'm really spooky!

I'm called Ben,
I live with a hen,
Barbie loves Ken
And so does Jen!

I'm called Ali,
I live in a valley,
I like to play Rally
And in a dark alley!

Freddie Jones (8)
Otterton Primary School

I Am A Dolphin

I am a dolphin
A very pretty dolphin
I like to play and I like to sway
I am a naughty dolphin
I am going to pass and play
To stay with you
To stay with you
To stay with you
I've got a sparkling eye
I've got a happy smile
I might be shy because I'm only nine.

Saski Farrington (7)
Otterton Primary School

Cheeky Cheetah

I am a cheeky cheetah,
I've got a naughty smile.
Come and catch me if you can,
Then I'll run for a mile!
When I was little,
I was a wild child.
But now that I am older,
I'm bold and meek and mild.
My dad is very bad,
My mum has a very big bum.
My sister has a blister,
Right in the middle of her tum.
My baby brother is annoying,
My mum just says, 'Typical boys,'
When she has to buy him lots of toys!
My family is crazy
As you can see.
But they are not
As mad
As me!

Pippa Glanville (8)
Otterton Primary School

I Wish I Was . . .

I wish I was a big, blue whale gliding the through the sea,
I wish I was a chimpanzee swinging from tree to tree,
I wish I was a horse in the countryside,
I wish I was an eagle who could glide,
I wish I was a dragon breathing fire everywhere,
I wish I was a seal swimming with no cares,
But most of all I wish I was myself.

Samuel Smith (8)
Otterton Primary School

Naughty Cow

I'm a cow
Come play with me now
I like doing bows
As well as annoying owls
I had to vow to steal no more
Otherwise the police would make me poor!
I kicked down someone's door
And then I killed a wild boar
I hid someone's hat
And harmed a bat
I have a pet cat
I bought the cat a mat!
I've seen a shark
Who's scared of the dark!
Now it's time to end my poem,
All the audience are now going!

Tom Dufall (7)
Otterton Primary School

Little Elephant

I'm a little elephant, stamp go my feet,
Stamp, stamp, stamp, stamp, stamp, go my feet.

I stamp down the street and say *hi* to people I meet,
Then I go to the shop and buy something to eat.

I'm a clumsy little elephant, I squash everyone flat,
And yesterday a bat was sleeping in my hat!

I am an everlasting elephant, stamping through the trees,
Everyone looks up then they all tease me.

I am a happy, little elephant, stamping all around,
I can reach the sky but I can't touch the ground.

Hannah Hawkins (8)
Otterton Primary School

Sly Fox!

I'm a fox, I'm so sly,
Watch me as I pass by.
All the little vixens look up at me,
As I show off my good looks
And run and jump and flee!
I'm a proud, loud fox,
I'm quick on my feet,
I can run and jump but I can't climb trees!
I stay in my den all snuggled up tight,
I sleep in daylight but come out at night.
I trash up all the dustbins and jump upon my prey.
As soon as I have caught it,
I'll drag it far away.
I cannot hop
But when cars come I'll stop
In the middle of the road,
Just to let them know
I don't take the green cross code
And . . . oh no,
Ohhh!
I wish I was a cat,
Cos then I would have nine lives
But I'm glad I don't have nine wives,
But I guess I missed my chance, mate,
Maaate, maaate, mmmm!

Emily Keliher (7)
Otterton Primary School

I'm A Cat

I'm a cat with a hat
I love to have a pat.
I've got gleaming eyes
With a wiggly tail
And my teeth are as sharp as a knife.

Bradley Hayman (7)
Otterton Primary School

I'm Not An Elephant

I'm a honey-brown hamster,
I live in a damster.
I'm small but fast,
I wanna go back in the past.
I have short eyesight,
I say I might, I might, I might.
I am fat and fluffy,
My owner is called Tufty!
I've got a bit of white,
I fly a kite.
I'm gonna run away,
But not today.
I'm always naughty,
But I never get caughty.
I'm always hungry,
I can scare a monkey!
Chocolate is poisonous,
I don't like noisiness!
Now it is time to say bye, bye,
Please don't cry
Or I will start saying, 'My, my, my, my, my!'

Sarah Brown (8)
Otterton Primary School

Flaming Firebird

As he swoops through the air
And he has fair hair
He is a flaming firebird and he is pretty hot
He is a flaming firebird and he is pretty hot
He swoops through the air as he swoops through the fire
He is a flaming firebird and he is pretty hot.

Hayden McDonald (8)
Otterton Primary School

Frog For A Day

If I were a frog,
I'd live in a pond,
And wear a David Beckham wig so blonde.

I'd sit on a lily pad,
With my very cool dad.

I'd jump into the water,
For an hour and a quarter.

I'd play all day,
Trampolining on the water,
Saying, 'Ribbit, ribbit, ribbit!'

Callum Archibald (7)
Otterton Primary School

The Cheeky, Cheeky Chimpanzee Poem

I'm a cheeky, cheeky chimpanzee
Watch me sliding through the trees
Stealing people's packed lunches.
He! He! He! He!
Stop it, you cheeky, cheeky chimpanzee.
I'll get him. Bang!
A rustle of leaves, a lot of fur
And that was the end of cheeky old me.
He! He! He!

Scott Hill (8)
Otterton Primary School

Untitled

I am a dog
I can't eat a frog.
I am a dog
I'm stuck in a log.
I am a cat
I think I swallowed a bat.
I am a fly
Touch me and die.

Jake Baker
Otterton Primary School

The Fair

First I'm on the roller coaster
Round and round the bend,
I'm starting to feel giddy
When the ride comes to an end.

Next I'm on the carousel
As we go around
I'm going higher and higher,
Until my feet can't reach the ground.

Then I go on the helter-skelter
I'm sliding down very fast
Faster and faster,
Shame that ride didn't last.

Last I go on the Ferris wheel
Upside down I go
Then suddenly the ride stops,
And I'm stuck in the air - oh no!

Rebecca Lawrence (11)
Roselands Primary School

Be Calm

The day is Palm Sunday
All I want to do is be calm
Sit on the beach and relax
Hear the waves lapping onto
The shore.

Feeling as if I was in a dream
Floating across the sea
I sit in my chair sunbathing
While the sun blazed down
On me!

Picking up a handful of sand
It just slips through my fingers.
Palm trees swaying in the breeze
While it ruffles my hair.

Siân Lenthall (10)
Roselands Primary School

Dogs

Dogs are very fun
They love to run and run
Mine, he sits on the floor
And his paw opens the door.

He is the best
And he's a pest
He acts like he is from the
Wild West.

Lauren Dawkins (9)
Roselands Primary School

My Funny Class

Becky is annoying
She sings a bit too much
If she doesn't shut up
Jade'll hit her with a clutch.

Sam's not cool
He chats up the girls
But he's not very good at it
So he makes them hurl.

Jamie is tall
Hannah is small
Nathan is fast
And Lauren is last.

Ben's my friend
His name rhymes with hen
He's quite intelligent
And has got a blue fountain pen.

Stuart is cool
He's kinda lazy
He is a footy-maniac
And his hair is really crazy.

Dan is my best friend
He doesn't give up
He tries to run really fast
But it's time for sup.

Ryan Morey (10)
Roselands Primary School

Lizard

There was a lizard
Who was lost
In a blizzard
He thought
He had no gizzard.

Lauren Thomas (8)
Roselands Primary School

Football

Football is a sport
A sport that I would enjoy.

Football is a sort
Of game that I enjoy.

Football is a thing
That I like to sing
About!

Conor Morey (7)
Roselands Primary School

Food

Food, food, I like food
Bananas, apples
Oranges and pears!
All delicious fruits.

Food, food, I like food
Carrots, potatoes,
Broccoli and peas.
All delicious veg!

Cory Stephenson (8)
Roselands Primary School

Birthday Wishes

A year of laughter
A bundle of fun
Chasing those giggles
Out in the sun
Dreaming a dream
When the day is done.

Tarah Courtenay (9)
Roselands Primary School

Nature's Song

Nature's song begins in the morning,
When spring's dew has set.
When the birds and trees awake,
When you go to feed your pet.

It continues on throughout the day,
Singing about everything.
Humans can hear it but they just don't listen,
But I listen, I love how it sings.

Prowling through the silent forest,
Even the song stops dead.
The fox spots its prey, beyond a tree,
A soft, white, fluffy head.

The unsuspecting rabbit,
Twitches its nose and sniffs.
It turns its head and sees the fox,
It runs, it's very swift.

The rabbit's still running into the flowers,
The fox follows, they both disappear.
Human voices calling to home,
They say, 'He's over there.'

The song has started again,
The children pick up the cat.
The cat is small and fluffy,
In its paws it clutches a rat.

Suddenly out leaps a dog,
A big, bushy dog with a big, brown snout.
'Don't hurt him, Rover!'
The children shout.

The song still continues,
But carefully slows down.
As the black of night draws over,
The song stops, not a sound.

Sam Frost (10)
Roselands Primary School

Summer

Summer is a season
Summer is a month
Summer is just the best!

Summer is the time when the sun comes out
It is always very hot.
Don't forget to put cream on
Otherwise you'll get sunburnt.

Summer is a season
Summer is a month
Summer is the time when the days get long.

Summer is a season
Summer is a month
Summer is just the best!

Craig Barton (9)
Roselands Primary School

Parents

Parents, they have so many rules.
Don't do this.
Don't do that.
Why don't you shut up?

Make my bum as sore as you want
But you're not gonna get me to wear that thing, you old hag.

I hate you, I hate you,
Why don't you let me pierce my bellybutton
Or get a tattoo?

I know you love me really
But you still know I'm moving out when I'm fifteen.

Jade Marie Coram (10)
Roselands Primary School

Rugby

Rugby's rough,
Rugby's tough,
Some rugby players go off in a huff.
Martin Johnson got the cuffs
Because the ref had had enough.

Jonny Wilko and his boot
When he gets the chance he'll shoot!
Old Matt Dawson you count to two
Give him the chance and he'll be through!

Finally it's Sir Clive Wood
Who leads his team to glory
And the World Cup goods.
But then of course came the nation's loss!
It was violent France
Who won the winning toss.

Samuel Parker (9)
Roselands Primary School

Football

1. Football is good.
2. Football is funny.
3. Football is cool.
4. Football is fun.
5. Football is crazy.
6. Football is nice.
7. Football is good.
8. Football is terrific.
9. I like football.
10. Do you like football?
11. Football is wicked.
12. Football is mad!

Michael Anning (8)
Roselands Primary School

France

France only comes in one kind
France you can easily find
France has a flag with white, red and blue
France isn't very new!

France is alright
It doesn't bite!
You can go there at night
Or you can go in the light!

France is very nice
It doesn't have lice
France is flying on a kite
It's a very pretty sight!

France is a very nice place
The people there
Always have a smile on their face.
France can talk in *French!*

Claire Brooking (9)
Roselands Primary School

The Tongue Twister

I'm going to write a tongue twister.
A tongue twister there will be!
With a pop twister and a lollipop microphone
You can sing to me!

Tomorrow Tilly tells the tongue twister,
Today Tilly touches her toes,
Tomorrow Tilly tells the tongue twister,
Today Tilly tastes Tom's tomatoes!

Krystina Murray (9)
Roselands Primary School

Best Friends

With your best friends you can laugh, shout and be silly.
Your best friend is like they're part of your family.
They have fun all the time.
They even invite you to their party.
They get you out of danger.
Don't forget they always play football.

Stewart Darke (11)
Roselands Primary School

Day And Night

Day is a lively place
Surrounded by people
Storming buildings tower above me
I'm scared, frightened of the day.

Night is a calming place
You can relax and go to sleep
I'm not frightened of the night
But I guess the day is quite alright!

Chloè-Sharn Dorrell (11)
Roselands Primary School

A Riddle

I practically have four legs and eyes.
I could be a bed but not very often.
If someone saw me it could damage their eyes.
I've been in the wars with a lot of my kind.

What am I?

A car.

Ivan Strul (11)
Roselands Primary School

Rugby

England are the best
They're better than the rest
Jonny is the hero
The other teams are zero
They can kick the balls so high
Then go back for some pie
We won the World Cup
But it wasn't just luck
Now you know rugby
It has been told
Don't support the other teams
They are so old.

Marcus O'Hara (10)
Roselands Primary School

Food

When eating food
You have to be rude!
I brought some food to the party
We did some karate!
We go to the fair
I ate a pear there!

I ate a carrot
As bright as a parrot!
I ate a pea
As small as a flea!
When eating food
You have to be rude!

Campbell Dougherty (8)
Roselands Primary School

School

My school is the best
In all of the rest
Everyone wants to go there
They are mad, they are silly
They are madder than me.

All the teachers are funny
Especially Mr Ellis
He makes the children laugh
When they are in a mood especially.

When they are sad and bored
The work always makes them have good fun
They are noisy, they always have lunch crisps.

When the clock ticks one, everyone tries their best in class
They even learn more when the teacher talks.

Chloe Gibbons (9)
Roselands Primary School

Toys

You break a toy
You snap a toy
You fix a toy!
You play with a toy
You notice a toy
You mix a toy!

Amber Hodgson (9)
Roselands Primary School

I Walked Down The Hill

I walked down the hill
I met a boy called Bill
He was very ill
And so he took a pill!
When he was walking down the hill
He wore a frill
But he had a little chill!
Then he saw Lill
Lill was ill
She had a chill
She wore a frill like Bill.

Callan Fadian (7)
Roselands Primary School

My Cat Was Fat

My cat
Was fat
He wore
A hat
He liked
His hat
'Cause it
Was fat
Yes it
Was fat
Like the
Cat!

Paige Elford (8)
Roselands Primary School

The Lizard Song

Neither hair nor shell have I
But I have four legs and a tail
And I change
Colour, colour, colour.

Neither fur nor claws have I
But I have scales but I don't swim
And I change
Colour, colour, colour.

I'm the master of all movement
And I can crawl, jump and leap
And I switch
Colours, colours, colours.

Natalie Crockford (10)
St Mary's CE Primary School, Truro

The Chameleon Song

Neither fur nor feathers have I,
But I have four knobbly legs and a coiled tail,
And I can *change, change, change!*
Neither spots nor stripes have I,
But I have giant, coloured, bulbous eyes,
And I can *change, change, change!*
I master every movement,
For I slowly crawl, climb and silently chew,
And I will *change, change, change!*

Emma Bolt (10)
St Mary's CE Primary School, Truro

The Owl Song

Neither silky fur nor silver scales have I,
But I have powerful wings to fly up high,
And I can hunt, hunt, hunt!

Neither smooth fins nor a hard shell have I,
But I have large eyes so I can spy,
And I can hunt, hunt, hunt!

I master every movement,
For I soar, swerve and glide,
And I cruelly
Hunt, hunt, hunt!

Sophie Evans (10)
St Mary's CE Primary School, Truro

The Jellyfish Song

Neither matted fur nor soft hair have I
But I have a body made of wobbly jelly
And I can sting, sting, sting!

Neither slimy scales nor colourful feathers have I
But I float almost weightlessly in the water
And I can sting, sting, sting.

I master every movement
For I glide, float, swim and scare
And I like to sting, sting, sting!

Amanda Louise Richards (10)
St Mary's CE Primary School, Truro

Summer

S un kissed children having a lot of fun,
U ntouched lolly already melted by the sun.
M oney spent on hire boats for the kids,
M emories made, like Amy's first step in a sun washed cave.
E xtra treats in the arcade, rally car, dance machines,
R eally don't want to go, but we have to. Bye.

Kate Ashton (10)
St Mary's CE Primary School, Truro

From A Railway Carriage

There is a cook, boiling his dinner,
Here is a lady, who is a singer.
There is a car, stuck in the bus's way,
Here are two children, going out to play.
In that garden, there is a tree,
In that garden, there is a bee.
There is a boy, who always tries,
There is a girl, who always cries.

Kensa Knuckey (10)
St Mary's CE Primary School, Truro

Summer

S pring has gone, summer's here
U tterings of cold, winter days have disappeared
M int choc chip ice creams around children's faces
M igrating birds fly to hot places
E nergetic children running
R ound the beach, rabbits sitting on your lap
   clinging like a leech.

Tegan Endean (10)
St Mary's CE Primary School, Truro

The Turtle Song!

Neither a scale nor smooth hair have I
But I have four small legs and one large head but no arms
And I slowly
Waddle, waddle, waddle!

Neither small nor thin am I
But I hide in my big shell on my strong, rough back
And I slowly
Waddle, waddle, waddle!

I master every movement
For I stop, bang and walk
And pleasantly
Waddle, waddle, waddle!

Bethany Willson (10)
St Mary's CE Primary School, Truro

The Cheetah Song

Neither hooves nor beak have I
But I have blotchy spots and sharp claws
And I am the
Fastest, fastest, fastest.

Neither slippery flippers nor bushy mane have I
But I have smooth fur and a brilliant eye
And I am the
Fastest, fastest, fastest.

I master every movement
For I leap, jump and pounce
And I am by far the
Fastest, fastest, fastest.

Bria Fay (10)
St Mary's CE Primary School, Truro

The Tiger Song

Neither rough trunk nor smooth ivory have I
But I have four legs and a tail
And I can
Kill, kill, kill!

Neither colourful spots nor manky slime have I
But I don't live in water
And I can kill, kill, kill!

I master every movement
For I quickly sprint, swift climbing and hunting
And I constantly
Kill, kill, kill!

Kara Boothby (10)
St Mary's CE Primary School, Truro

The Cheetah Song

Neither clumping hooves nor smooth shoes have I
But I have a tail, sharp teeth and spots
And I can
Run, run, run!

Neither a deep pouch nor strong shell have I
But I have long legs and yellow ears
And I can
Run, run, run!

I master every movement
For I crawl, walk and sprint
And I rapidly
Sprint, sprint, sprint!

Daniel Peter Ballett (10)
St Mary's CE Primary School, Truro

The Tortoise Song!

Neither fur nor scales have I
But I have four legs and no arms
And I move
Slowly, slowly, slowly!

Neither fins nor feathers have I
But I have one large shell
And I move
Slowly, slowly, slowly!

I master every movement
For I waddle slowly and swim
And ramble
Slowly, slowly, slowly!

Emma Unwin (9)
St Mary's CE Primary School, Truro

The Elephant Song

Neither big hooves nor small shoes have I
But I have huge ears and rough grey skin
And I can
Stomp, stomp, stomp!

Neither small spots nor big stripes have I
But I make a loud noise to scare enemies away
And I can
Stomp, stomp, stomp!

I master every movement
For I travel, remember and blow water
And I loudly
Stomp, stomp, stomp!

Laura Ann Thomas (10)
St Mary's CE Primary School, Truro

Summer

S ummer sand that's boiling hot.
U seless, horrible, cloudy weather.
M elting chocolate down toddler's faces.
M eeting lots of new people in the summery street.
E ating crunchy, juicy salad.
R unning around on the silky sand.

Sian Williams (10)
St Mary's CE Primary School, Truro

Summer

S and and sun are very beautiful
U nder the sand are little bugs
M elted ice cream dripping down to the feet
M oney spent on spoilt children, money galore they certainly
call it.
E verlasting sun today.
R eally sorry, we've got to fly away.

Aarron Ingleby-Oddy (10)
St Mary's CE Primary School, Truro

Summer

S un shining on the window, sand on our faces.
U nless it's cloudy and is raining.
M uttering children not wanting to go out.
M orning sunshine waking you up very early.
E ventually sitting on the beach watching the waves come in
and out.
R unning through the huge waves that knock you down.

Harry-James Henley (9)
St Mary's CE Primary School, Truro

The Cheetah Song

Neither web nor powerful guns have I
But I have hairy fur and paws
And I can
Run, run, run!

Neither hands nor huge shoes have I
But I have feet with huge claws
And I can
Run, run, run!

I master every movement
For I run to catch and pounce
And I can
Run, run, run!

Richard Mercer (9)
St Mary's CE Primary School, Truro

The Fish Song

Neither legs nor arms have I
But I have an underwater tail
And I blow
Bubbles, bubbles, bubbles.

Neither hair nor fur have I
But I have eyes in the side of my head
And I blow
Bubbles, bubbles, bubbles.

I master every movement
For I swim, dive and eat
And I swim
Deeper, deeper, deeper.

Samantha Tregunna (9)
St Mary's CE Primary School, Truro

The Cheetah Song

Neither sharp fangs nor poisonous venom have I
But I have spots and claws
And I run
Faster, faster, faster!

Neither flashy scales nor hard shell have I
But I have a long, furry tail
And I run
Faster, faster, faster!

I master every movement
For I run, pounce and prey
And I fiercely
Pounce, pounce, pounce!

Alexander Caddy (10)
St Mary's CE Primary School, Truro

Creepy Crawly Insects

Creepy crawly insects,
Ladybirds, butterflies,
Creepy crawly insects.

They can be crawly,
Or creepy,
They lay eggs,
Creepy crawly insects.

Some eat other insects,
Some eat plants,
Some eat leaves,
Creepy crawly insects.

Creepy crawly insects,
Creepy crawly insects,
Bees, dragonflies,
Creepy crawly insects!

Chelsea Letcher (8)
St Mewan CP School, St Austell

The Moon

Gaze up high,
Into space,
Peeping down,
A friendly face.

The full moon is like
A white eyeball staring up to Heaven,
An old, dusty mirror showing silent shadows.

Gaze up high,
Above tall trees,
Changing now,
A letter C.

The crescent moon is like
A white banana in a gloomy mouth,
A cream beak pecking the starry sky.

Gaze up high,
The moon is sad,
Out comes the sun,
Feeling so glad.

Daniel Jordan Berry (9)
St Mewan CP School, St Austell

Sampan

Waves lap, lap
Fish fins slap, slap
Brown sails rap, rap
Chopsticks snap, snap
I can feel the river flowing
Sampan, sampan
Waves lap, lap
Fish fins slap, slap
Brown sails rap, rap
Chopsticks snap, snap.

Charlotte Cutlan (8)
St Mewan CP School, St Austell

Senses Poem

Listen!
What can you hear?
The sound of my cat scratching against the door.
The sound of the lambs up on the moor.
Touch!
What can you feel?
The texture in my fluffy fleece.
The warm skin on my little niece.
Look!
What can you see?
The calm weather outside.
The crashing waves on the tide.
Lick!
What can you taste?
The lovely taste of food.
The person who makes it is usually in a bad mood.
Sniff!
What can you smell?
The smell of chips and lemons with no pips.

Ashleigh Hellier (8)
St Mewan CP School, St Austell

Senses

Touch!
What can you feel?
The velvety feathers of a newborn chick.
The icy-cold flippers of a cute, baby penguin.

Touch!
What can you feel?
The prickly, pointy leaves of a palm tree.
The soft, furry cotton of my multicoloured jumper.

Georgia Parkin-Jones (7)
St Mewan CP School, St Austell

The Moon

Gaze up high,
Into space.
Peeping down,
A friendly face.

The full moon is like
A tired eye spying on me.
The full moon is like
A smiley face staring at me.

Gaze up high,
Above tall trees.
Changing now,
A letter C.

The crescent moon is like
A swaying hammock in the sky.
The crescent moon is like a ripe banana lying in the dark.

Tom Westlake (9)
St Mewan CP School, St Austell

Stuck In Bed

My name is Edd
I'm stuck in my bed
Because I've hurt my head.

My name is Edd
And I'm stuck in my red,
Yucky, smelly bed.

My name is Edd
And my friend is Fred
And he bumped his head.

My name is Edd
I'm stuck in my bed
Because I've hurt my head.

Hayley Watts (8)
St Mewan CP School, St Austell

Listen

Listen!
What can you hear?
The moo of the cows in the field
The wheels of the car on the road.
Touch!
What can you feel?
The soft cream of the cake
The lovely, green grass on the ground.
Look!
What can you see?
The clear, blue sky in the air
The bright, yellow sun.
Lick!
What can you taste?
The sour, yellow lemon off the tree
The ripe, green apple from the tree.
Sniff!
What can you smell?
The smell of my Cheerios in the morning
The smell of the cheese in the fridge.

Luke Perkes (8)
St Mewan CP School, St Austell

Growing Plants Poem

Plants grow everywhere,
They can be weeds,
Or they can grow from seeds.
Tiny plants, huge plants,
Where would we be without plants?
Beautiful plants, beautiful plants,
They can dance, oh, dance, oh, dance.
Plants, plants, what will you do?
Plants didlly didlly doo.

Bethany Martin (8)
St Mewan CP School, St Austell

The Moon

Gaze up high,
Into space.
Peeping down,
A friendly face.

The full moon is like
A tired eye staring at me.
The full moon is like a singing mirror
Resting in a bedroom.

Gaze up high,
Above tall trees.
Changing now,
A letter C.

The crescent moon is like
A sharp claw scratching the blackboard.
The crescent moon is like
A yummy melon going into your mouth.

Deanna Paull (8)
St Mewan CP School, St Austell

If You Want To See A Condor

If you want to see a Condor
You must go up to the lonely Mongu Mountains
Or the Himabreian valleys
But you'd better take care because
The mountains are slippery
And the valleys are slippery.
If you want to see a Condor
You must say swooping Condor
Swooping Condor
Swooping Condor
And clap your hands twice
And she will catch the wind down onto the earth
But you'd better take care because
That Condor pecks people.

Zachary Vaughan (8)
St Mewan CP School, St Austell

Senses

Listen!
What can you hear?
I can hear a dog
Barking loudly from a cage.
Touch!
What can you feel?
I can feel a quilt
That is made of wool.
Look!
What can you see?
I can see a football
Falling down from the sky.
Lick!
What can you taste?
I can taste Spaghetti Bolognese
That came out from the hot oven.
Sniff!
What can you smell?
I can smell smoke,
Burning sticks from an old tree.

Alex Perkes (8)
St Mewan CP School, St Austell

I'm Bored!

I'm bored sat by this wall.
I'm watching my brother play football.
What can I do?
I'd much rather go to the zoo.
I'm bored!

How much more boring can this get?
This is dull, especially when it's wet.
I would have brought my coat if I knew,
I've got nothing to *do!*
I'm bored!

I am so bored!
They've still got half the match left
Please blow the whistle, come on, ref!
It's nearly finished now.
Oh dear, someone's done a foul.
I don't care, I'm just bored, of course.
I'm very, very bored!
I'm bored!
I'm bored!
I'm bored!
I'm bored!

Lucy Lund (8)
St Mewan CP School, St Austell

The Changing Moon

Gaze up high
Into space
Peeping down,
A loving face.

The full moon is like
A beaming eye,
Spying on the world.
The full moon is like
A silver marble,
Rolling up to Heaven.

Gaze up high,
Above the tall trees.
Changing now,
A letter C.

The crescent moon is like
A razor-sharp claw
Clinging high in the sky.
The crescent moon is like
A rowing boat sailing
To the stars.

Gaze up high
See it float.
Changing now,
A sailing boat.

Grace Nichole Digweed (9)
St Mewan CP School, St Austell

The Changing Moon

Gaze up high,
Into space.
Spying down,
A cheerful face.

The full moon is like
A changeable disco ball swirling above the clouds.
The full moon is like
A working elbow bone wobbling around the world.

Gaze up high,
See it float.
Changing now,
A sailing boat.

The crescent moon is like
A ripe banana making me peckish.
The crescent moon is like
A relaxed letter C trying to sleep.

Gaze up high,
Staring down.
A cheeky smile,
Has been found.

Hannah Kendall (9)
St Mewan CP School, St Austell

The Changing Moon

Gaze up high,
Into space.
Peeping down,
A friendly face.

The full moon is like
A glistening marble rolling down a desk.
The full moon is like
A silver coin twinkling in the night.

Gaze up high,
Above tall trees.
Changing now,
So come and see.

The crescent moon is like
A ripe banana making me peckish.
The crescent moon is like
A cheeky smile avoiding trouble.

Gaze up high,
Look and see.
A shining pearl,
Above the trees.

Charlotte Ann Kiddy (9)
St Mewan CP School, St Austell

Changing Moon

Gaze up high,
Into space.
Glancing down,
A cheerful face.

The full moon is like
A round, old clock
On a black, tattered wall.
A wide-open eye
Staring down to Earth.

Gaze up high,
Above tall trees.
Changing now
A letter C.

The crescent moon is like
An upset frown,
Crying raindrops,
A swishing boat,
Sailing to stars.

Gaze up high,
To the sky
And watch it disappear.
The sun will rise,
The moon will have gone.
Finally all clear.

Sarah Roberts (9)
St Mewan CP School, St Austell

The Full Moon And Crescent Moon

Gaze up high,
Into space.
Peeping down,
A friendly face.

The full moon is like
A gleaming pearl
Spying around the atmosphere.
A coloured marble smashing like glass.

Gaze up high,
Above tall trees.
Changing now,
A letter C.

The crescent moon is like
A killer tooth glistening in the moonlight
And last but not least a razor-sharp claw
Scraping on a blackboard.

Charlie Andrew French (8)
St Mewan CP School, St Austell

The Moon

Gaze up high
In space
Peeping down
A friendly face.

The full moon is like
A Malteser.
The moon is like
A twinkling star.

Gaze up high
Above tall trees.
Changing now,
A letter C.

The crescent moon is like
A smiley mouth.
The crescent moon is like
A slice of an apple.

Matthew Wellington (8)
St Mewan CP School, St Austell

Changing Moon

Gaze up high,
Into space.
Peeping down,
A friendly face.

The full moon is like
A magical, crystal ball
Showing the future.
The full moon is like
A yummy gobstopper
Sparkling in space.

Gaze up high,
Above tall trees.
Changing now,
A letter C.

The crescent moon is like
A crowded ship
Swaying in space.
The crescent moon is like
A razor-sharp claw
Ripping the atmosphere.

Gaze up high,
Staring down.
The moon is sad,
Like a tired frown.

Adam Allerton (9)
St Mewan CP School, St Austell

The Changing Moon

Gaze up high,
Into space.
Peeping down,
A friendly face.

The full moon is like
An ancient Greek coin in a museum.
The full moon is like
A rolling marble racing around the desk.

Gaze up high,
Above tall trees.
Changing now,
A letter C.

The crescent moon is like
A hungry tooth munching the stars.
The crescent moon is like
A furious frown seeing naughty things.

Gaze up high,
Into the day.
Seeking down
Driving away.

Amy D Sweet (9)
St Mewan CP School, St Austell

The Moon

Gaze up high,
Into space,
Peeping down,
A friendly face.

The full moon is like
A shining button glowing in the sky,
A glittering marble rolling on the track.

Gaze up high,
Above tall trees,
Changing now,
A letter C.

The crescent moon is like
A half-eaten Jaffa Cake
Floating through the sky.
A broken rib in a sleeping body.

Gaze up high,
Morning is nigh.
Sun is coming,
Time to fly!

Tessa Marie Isted (8)
St Mewan CP School, St Austell

The Changing Moon

Gaze up high,
Into space,
Peeping down,
A caring face.

The full moon is like
A bouncy ball spinning to the stars,
A prehistoric coin stuffed in my trouser pocket.

Gaze up high,
Above tall trees,
Changing now,
A letter C.

The crescent moon is like
A juicy melon slice hopping into the sky's blue mouth,
A rocking boat flowing to Heaven.

Gaze up high,
To the stars,
Peeping down,
Just below Mars.

Lucy Rothero (9)
St Mewan CP School, St Austell

The Amazing Moon

Gaze up high,
Into space.
Peeping down,
A friendly face.

The full moon is like a
Streaking party balloon
Tied to a chair.
The full moon is like a
Black and white football
Shooting through the goal.

Gaze up high,
Above tall trees.
Changing now,
A letter C.

The crescent moon is like a
Juicy melon slice
Watering in my mouth.
The crescent moon is like a
Crunchy, curly chip
Lying on my tongue.

Gaze up high,
Take a peep.
Pointing down,
A cactus leaf.

Victoria Cocks (9)
St Mewan CP School, St Austell

The Extraordinary Moon

Gaze up high
Into space
Peeping down
A caring face.

The full moon is like
A magical, crystal ball
Showing the future,
A shining pearl spying
Down on Earth.

Gaze up high
Above tall trees
Changing now
A letter C.

The crescent moon is like
A caterpillar curling up in sleep
A rowing boat
Sailing through the galaxy.

Gaze up high
Into the clouds
Where in Heaven?
Beyond the crowd.

Jenna Trudgeon (9)
St Mewan CP School, St Austell

The Full Moon And The Crescent Moon

Gaze up high,
Into space.
Peeping down,
A friendly face.

The full moon is like
A yummy, white Malteser popping into my mouth.
The full moon is like
A whizzing basketball scoring a goal.

Gaze up high,
Above tall trees.
Changing now,
A letter C.

The crescent moon is like
A bendy horn poking my bottom.
The crescent moon is like
A whirly, curly chip floating around above my head.

Gaze up high,
To see the moon.
Spying down,
Like a balloon.

Samuel Joseph Moore (9)
St Mewan CP School, St Austell

The Moon

Gaze up high,
Into space,
Peeping down,
A friendly face.

The full moon is like
A prehistoric coin lying in a museum.
The full moon is like a huge wedding cake sitting on a table.

Gaze up high,
Above tall trees,
Changing now.
A letter C.

The crescent moon is like
A cheeky smile trying to avoid trouble.
The crescent moon is like
A juicy melon slice oozing water.

Gaze up high,
Which moon can you see?
Is the crescent there?
It's bound to be.

Rachel Nottle (8)
St Mewan CP School, St Austell

The Magical Moon

Gaze up high
Into space
Peeping down
A friendly face.

The full moon is like
A misty, crystal ball
Showing the future . . .

The full moon is like
A hedgehog snuggled
Into a coil . . .

Gaze up high
Above tall trees
Changing now
A letter C.

The crescent moon is like
A wriggling worm
Plodding into space

The crescent moon is like
A scraping claw cutting me.

Gaze up high
By the moon
Staring down
A peaceful tune.

Thomas Snell (8)
St Mewan CP School, St Austell

The Crystal Moon

Gaze up high
Into space
Peeping down
A friendly face.

The crystal moon is like
An antique coin lying in an unfound chest.

The crystal moon is like
A spinning globe whizzing round the Earth.

Gaze up high
Above tall trees
Changing now
A letter C.

The crescent moon is like
A wriggly worm squirming through the galaxy.

The crescent moon is like
A squidgy banana popping in space.

Gaze up high
Above the world
Spying on Earth
A claw so curled.

Elliot James Baker (8)
St Mewan CP School, St Austell

The Coated Moon

Gaze up high,
Into space.
Peeping down,
A friendly face.

The moon is like
A coated Malteser glistening
In the night sky.

The full moon is like
A sleepy caterpillar curled
Among yellow stars.

Gaze up high,
Above tall trees.
Changing now,
A letter C.

The crescent moon is like
A swaying ship sparkling
In the blue sky.

The crescent moon is like
A bruised banana showing
A miserable face.

Alicia Smerdon (9)
St Mewan CP School, St Austell

The Moon

Gaze up high,
Into space.
Peeping down,
A friendly face.

The full moon is like
A yummy Malteser.
The full moon is like
A funny face with eyes.

Gaze up high,
Above the trees.
Changing now,
A letter C.

The crescent moon is like
A pecking beak hammering a tree.

The crescent moon is like
A juicy melon slice watering in my mouth.

Christopher Allen (9)
St Mewan CP School, St Austell

Fairies

F riends and fairies playing,
A nd always sharing food,
I always give them teeth,
R ound, red, juicy sweets,
I love fairies,
E ating is so much fun,
S o fairies never learn.

Tamsin Pritchard (8)
St Peter's CE Junior School, Tavistock

Rats

Rats can scurry,
Fast and slow,
Rats can hide high and low.

Rats can hide,
Under mats,
They also run away from cats.

Rats are small,
Rats are cool,
Rats can hide,
In swimming pools.

Rats come in all shapes and sizes,
They can give you such surprises,
Eating all the food in sight,
They can give you a real fright.

Daryl Panter (9)
St Peter's CE Junior School, Tavistock

In The Dark, Dark Woods

In the dark, dark woods
I had a spook
And in the dark, dark woods
Something jumped out of the bush
In the dark, dark woods
And in the dark, dark woods
I saw a man
In the dark, dark woods
He had a bag
I could not see what was in it
But it think it was real gold
In the dark, dark woods.

Emma Champion (8)
St Peter's CE Junior School, Tavistock

Who Are You?

Who are you?
Who are you?
What's your name?

Is it Tom?
Is it Dom?
Who are you?

Are you small?
Are you tall?
Who are you?

Tell me your name!
Are you tame?
Who are you?

Are you human?
Are you alien?
Who are you?

Where are you?
Are you there?
Under that chair?

Who are you?
Are you in my pocket?
Is that you?
Oh, will you stop it?

Luke McClung (8)
St Peter's CE Junior School, Tavistock

Best Friends

Best friends, best friends,
Our friendship never ends,
We always fall out
And make up again . . .
And very, very soon
We're all best friends.

Bethany Horton (7)
St Peter's CE Junior School, Tavistock

What Is Yellow?

What is yellow?
My hamster's yellow.
She always eats marshmallows.
What is red?
A rose is red
As a red lip to eat with.
What is blue?
The sky is blue
And the twinkling stars twinkle.
What is green?
The leaves are green
As nice, green jumpers.
What is orange?
The sky is orange
As the sun sets down.

Katie Bolt (8)
St Peter's CE Junior School, Tavistock

Screams In The Castle

Screams in the castle,
Must be a ghost.
Someone's being murdered,
Blood is everywhere.
Screaming in the castle,
Ghosts are all out now.
Better watch out
Or else you'll be dead!
Let's have a look
At the living dead.
So when it's very dark in your room
Watch out, there might be a boom
And in a flash of light
A headless lady, carrying babies will appear
With ginger, long hair right to the ground.
So you'd better watch out for the living dead!

Georgia Mary Bartlett (8)
St Peter's CE Junior School, Tavistock

A War Is Out There!

A war is out there,
A war is out there,
It sounds like a nightmare,
It sounds like a nightmare,
Here come the bombs,
Here come the bombs,
They sound like big gongs,
They sound like big gongs,
People running, people screaming
Out in the street it's a total *nightmare!*
A war is out there,
Men fighting for their lives,
People taking riskful dives,
Shouts of pain,
Shouts of pain,
You just might see the toss of a mane,
As the gunfire closes down,
You know it's the end of the war in this town.

Daniel Allan (8)
St Peter's CE Junior School, Tavistock

The Smugglers' Den

The smugglers are riding through the town,
Come on, pirates, get them down.
If you see those smugglers catch 'em in a net,
But if you do the pirate crew will have a bet at you.

Run, run, smugglers, run back to your den,
Never see the pirates again and never see their den.
The night has come, the sun's gone down,
See you in the morning.
In the morning they're still yawning.

Jacob Rose (9)
St Peter's CE Junior School, Tavistock

Are You There?

Are you there?
Are you there?
Are you there behind that chair?

Are you big?
Are you small?
Is that a sound I hear you call?

Are you round?
Are you square?
Are you under this armchair?

Are you fat?
Are you thin?
Are you inside that bin?

Is that you?
It is too!
You're not round,
You're not square,
You're a pair of underwear!

Matthew Woodhouse (8)
St Peter's CE Junior School, Tavistock

My Family

My dad is grumpy
When he comes home from work.
My mum is lazy
When she comes home from work.
So we can't have our dinner until nine o'clock!

Timothy Davidson (8)
St Peter's CE Junior School, Tavistock

In The Morning

In the morning,
When I wake up,
I'm still yawning.
In the morning,
Get my book,
And read in the morning.
In the morning,
I rub my eyes.
In the morning,
Get up and find,
I'm still yawning.

Go downstairs,
In the morning,
And *still* find,
I'm still yawning.
Watch some TV,
In the morning,
And even now,
I'm still yawning.
Have some breakfast,
I'm still yawning.

Get ready for school,
In the morning,
And still I find,
I'm still yawning.
I tell everyone,
I can't stop yawning.

Laura Hooper (9)
St Peter's CE Junior School, Tavistock

Boring School

Once again, we're stuck in school,
Then we know, work isn't cool.
Now we're playing, playing, playing,
So then the whistle starts blowing, blowing.

Once again we're stuck in school,
Now swimming in a swimming pool.
Then we go on a trip,
Whoops-a-daisy, you've just slipped!

Once again we're stuck in school,
When we could be playing football.
So when we're having our nice lunch,
Then the teacher gives me a punch.

Once again we're stuck in school,
When we could be playing basketball.
So we get some homework.
Oh no! I forgot my work!

Josh Hosking (8)
St Peter's CE Junior School, Tavistock

Dinosaur

Little, tiny dinosaur,
Had a toe that was very sore.

Little, ginger and white cat,
Was actually incredibly fat.

Little, brown-coloured dog,
Looked a bit like a warthog.

Little, rather small, elephant,
Is not all that intelligent.

Samuel O'Boyle (8)
St Peter's CE Junior School, Tavistock

Chloe

Chloe is mad
Chloe is sad
Chloe is cool
Chloe loves the swimming pool
Chloe likes me very much
And she likes singing
Chloe loves the living room.

Francesca Lois White (7)
St Peter's CE Junior School, Tavistock

I Am The Song

I am the rocks that hit the sea
I am the tree that made the land
I am the song that made the bird sing
I am the soil that ate the worm
I am the nut that ate the squirrel
I am the ships that made the people
I am the room that lit the bulb.

Ryan Foster (11)
Salisbury Road Junior School

I Am The World

I am the songs that sing the bird.
I am the tide that shakes the land.
I am the mammal that grows on Earth.
I am the lake that carries the sand.
I am the wind that drives a twister.
I am the sun that puts out the eclipse.
I am the water that puts out a fire.
I am the earth that structured materials.
I am the world that built the man.

Andrew Clarke (10)
Salisbury Road Junior School

Britain At War

I remember the terrifying war:
Men picking up their rifles,
Sirens switching on so loudly.
I can feel the horror when the bombs drop on houses
As they collapse like an earthquake shaking.

I can hear the horrible screaming from miles away,
People trapped in burning houses like a guy on the bonfire
on Bonfire Night.
I can hear soldiers firing.
I can feel the wind swapping secrets as it passed through this
deserted town.
I think I would survive.

I look at the memorial stone.
I remember those who saved me and thank them for everything.
I can understand why they died
Yet pray that war will never be repeated again;
That no one died in vain.

John Hawkins (11)
Salisbury Road Junior School

Giant Bolster

Who owns this bristly-looking beard? Bolster
Who owns this 6-mile stride? Bolster
Who owns these bloodshot eyes? Bolster
Who owns this brown belt of cattle? Bolster
Who owns these scrawny feet? Bolster
Who owns this jagged knife? Bolster
All this shiny blood? Bolster
These crucified, bony children? Bolster
These bones of horror? Bolster
This chanting mouth? Bolster
Who bled to death? Bolster.

Josh Hall (10)
Tregadillett Community Primary School

Bolster

Who has a six-mile stride? Bolster.
Who carries cattle in his belt? Bolster.
Who is twelve miles high? Bolster.
Who fell in love with St Agnes? Bolster.
Who died for his marriage? Bolster.
Whose blood is still running down the cliff? Bolster.

All this gruesome blood? Bolster.
These staring, gloomy eyes? Bolster.
This bird's eye view? Bolster.

Stabbing, bleeding happening? Blood.

Who owns the scream of death? Bolster.
Who owns all of worlds? Bolster.
Who is weaker than St Agnes? Bolster.
Who is a ghost like him? Bolster.
Stronger than hate? Bolster.
Stronger than new? Bolster.
But who set Bolster a challenge? St Agnes.

Die, Bolster!

Ashton Oak (10)
Tregadillett Community Primary School

Giant Bolster

Who is taller than a fully-grown tree? Giant Bolster
Who can stride 6 miles? Giant Bolster
Who stole cattle and tied them to his belt? Giant Bolster
Who fell in love with St Agnes? Giant Bolster
Who tried a challenge that St Agnes sent him? Giant Bolster
Who left a long bloodstain of St Agnes' cliffs? Giant Bolster

But who set out to kill him?
St Agnes!

Siobhan Nelson (11)
Tregadillett Community Primary School

Mighty Monkey

I have seen the mighty monkey
swinging from tree to tree
I have heard his loud calling
that no one else can see.

I have watched the mighty monkey
feed on bugs and flies
I have touched the light brown fur
believe me, I tell no lies.

I have travelled through the day
until the morning light
I have climbed the spiky trees
and watched the monkeys fight.

I think the monkey liked me
although he soon will die
I tried to run and hide him
but then he caught someone's eye.

Then that someone shot him
right the way through his heart
although he will be near me
always in my heart.

Gemma Crook (11)
Tregadillett Community Primary School

Tiger Inn

Two strange tigers went to the inn,
One was yellow but the other was thin.

The lovely tigers had manes as pale,
As French paella or finest snail.

Where the tigers live it hails and snows.
The language they spoke nobody knows.

Ruby Griffiths (10)
Tregadillett Community Primary School

The Monster

Who has a six-mile-long stride?
Bolster
Who is twelve miles high?
Bolster
Who has sharp, red eyes?
Bolster
Who has a wicked, long stare?
Bolster
Who destroyed the countryside?
Bolster
Who caught cattle and tied them to his belt?
Bolster
Who fell in love with St Agnes?
Bolster
Who set Bolster an impossible task?
St Agnes
What did she say?
Go to the top of the cliffs and fill that pit with your blood.
Who didn't know that the pit was never-ending?
Bolster
Who bled to death?
Bolster.

Shane Sandercock (10)
Tregadillett Community Primary School

My Cornish Treasure Box

(Based on 'Magic Box' by Kit Wright)

In my Cornish treasure box I would put
The sound of spectacular surfing
The taste of rich pasties cooking in the shops
The bumpy feeling of the animals' bones
The sight of my childhood surroundings
The smell of golden treasure in the box.

Christopher Allen (11)
Tregadillett Community Primary School

The Sea Creatures

Up flies the whale
The largest of them all
He knocks against our foredeck
Saying, 'Here's fish for all.'
O praise the mighty whale
O swim far from shore
Our ship is still standing crew
How gentle she go!

Up flies the shark
The most fierce of all
He smacked against our foredeck
We could die all.

Then up crawls the crab
The smallest of all
He climbs on our foredeck
Saying, 'We shall survive all.'

Nikki Pannell (11)
Tregadillett Community Primary School

I Have Seen The Mighty Eagle

I have seen the mighty eagle
soaring over the blue sky,
he is king of all lands
because he will always fly.

Always flying from noon to night
his last trip is the big cliffs,
his first is the mountains,
his second is the snowdrifts.

He is the mighty eagle,
he roams over our skies,
he will always be our friend
a long time after he dies.

Lucy Griffiths (11)
Tregadillett Community Primary School

The Great Giant

Who is 12 miles long? *Bolster*
Who lives in a stone-cold cave? *Bolster*
Who has a stride of 6 miles long? *Bolster*
Who fell in love with St Agnes? *Bolster*
Who has a bird's eye view? *Bolster*
Who stole and broke villages? *Bolster*

All this red blood *Bolster*
These big, black eyes *Bolster*

Sacrificed his life *Bolster*
These manky, yellow nails *Bolster*

Left his mark wherever he went *Bolster*

Who is wicked and mean? *Bolster*
Whose blood ran into the sea? *Bolster*
Who had a belt of animals? *Bolster*
Who bled to death? *Bolster*
Not as strong as St Agnes *Bolster*
Has no life *Bolster*
But who is dead? *Bolster Bolster*.

Patsy Griffiths (11)
Tregadillett Community Primary School

The Star

There's a star in the sky
and it is shining bright
the pitch-blackness
in the middle of the night.

The star is magical
it has stories to teach
it's fallen from the sky
onto a long-lost beach.

Emma Hancock (10)
Tregadillett Community Primary School

The Lion

I have seen the lion among the gusty trees
The lion is a muscular figure
Dashing between rustling leaves.

Then the lion cries
For morning nighs
Closer and closer.

As it gallops through the boulders
Searching, searching
Searching for a place to hide
Then it halters.

For the soldiers went marching
Down, down
Dead went the lion with a thud
His body arching, arching.

I have seen the lion among the gusty trees
The lion is a ghostly figure
Tossed between cloudy seas.

Then it cries
For morning nighs
Closer and closer.

Daniel Petersen (10)
Tregadillett Community Primary School

The Woods

The woods are a wonderful place,
Full of happiness and grace,
Butterflies flutter and birds sing,
Everyone's joy for everything.

The sheep eat grass,
The badgers dig,
While the leaping squirrels,
Break the twigs.

The grass is green,
The mud is brown,
It's so peaceful,
Away from town.

In the woods,
There are thriving flowers,
In the centre,
The great beech towers.

It stands out,
From all the rest,
It quite simply,
Is the best.

Dale Wallington (9)
Tregadillett Community Primary School

Golden Eagle

I have followed the Golden Eagle,
I have searched low and high,
I have climbed craggy rocks,
And scanned the sky.

I have heard the Golden Eagle,
Screeching to the night air,
Echoing in the dark caves,
And the rocky ravines.

I have found the Golden Eagle,
On the rocks dead and cold,
He will screech no longer,
My heart is broken.

I have heard the Golden Eagle,
From the hollow of the ledge,
The eagle lives forever
In its warm, twig nest.

Sam Mercer (10)
Tregadillett Community Primary School

The Mean Giant

Who is a wicked giant? Bolster
Who is 12 miles tall? Bolster
Who has a 6-mile stride? Bolster
Who loves St Agnes? Bolster
Whose teeth are rotten? Bolster
Who slit himself with a knife? Bolster
Who tried to fill a pit with blood? Bolster
Who gave Bolster a challenge? St Agnes

Who hates Bolster? *Everyone!*

Die, Bolster, die.

Alexander Cornish (10)
Tregadillett Community Primary School

Death Calls Me

Up leaps the dolphin,
The brightest of the sea.
She jumps through the crashing waves,
She is calling for me.
O' crash the waves go,
O' crash the waves go.
They sound angry, they sound angry.

Up jumps the shark,
His gnashing jaws gnaw.
He jumped on our foredeck,
You'll live never more.

Then up clambers the crab,
The roughest of all.
He crawls on our foredeck,
You'll live never more.

Laura Dymond (11)
Tregadillett Community Primary School

The Blue Dolphins

I have heard of the blue dolphins,
I have swum through crashing waves,
I have voyaged over the swell,
And ran through sea caves.

I have traced the blue dolphins,
As each mighty splash,
As I followed the dolphins,
And watched the waves crash.

I have found the blue dolphins,
I looked low and high,
I have walked over sand,
Now he is mine.

Rebekka Wadland (11)
Tregadillett Community Primary School

The Woodland

I hear the woodland . . .

The squawking of the rooks.
The trickling of the stream.
The tweeting of the birds.
The humming of the bees.

I see the woodland . . .

The bluebells blooming in the blistering sun.
The rich, green colours of the leaves.
The shadow of the birds above me.
The squirrels in the trees.

I feel the woodland . . .

The serration of the fern stems.
The leathery feeling of the beech leaves.
The prickly feeling of the holly.
The bark of the old, oak trees.

Rebecca Pethers (11)
Tregadillett Community Primary School

The Indian

I have seen the Indian
I have ran far, far away
I have seen the amazing forest
It's a special place to stay.

I have heard the Indian
The rustling of the trees
With the nice, calm breeze
And the falling of the leaves.

I have spoken to the Indian
I heard her say,
'I am lost, I am lost
I'll decide which way.'

Melissa Marshall (11)
Tregadillett Community Primary School

Dartmoor Landscape

Gritting granite sticking to the stones.
Looking at the frozen sky.
Watching birds fly.
The stones huge with edges.

Grasslands steep, trees bushy.
Grass like straw.
Mud squidgy.

From the top of the tallest tor
I saw gritting granite
I saw rocks like sugar cubes
I saw a rock that looked like an eagle's head
I saw the frozen sky
I touched the spiky grass
I touched the water flowing in the river
I touched the misshapen rocks
I stared at the meander
I stared at the gigantic mountain.

Jordan Sheridan (10)
Victoria Road Primary School

Upon The Moor

Upon the moor on a misty morning,
I saw a piece of gritty granite lying on the floor.
I saw waterfalls like frothy shandy.
I saw the landscape, colourful in a dark way.

I touched the gigantic, jagged rocks.
I touched the grass that shook with the wind.

I heard the bluebirds barking in the distance.
I heard the green, green grass whistling in the wind.

Stacey Buckingham (11)
Victoria Road Primary School

Dartmoor!

Rushing rivers through the landscape.
Landscape with beautiful tors.
Tors are like tiny mountains.
Mountains are like camel humps on a camel's back.
Back to the rivers.
Rivers running far and wide.
Wide open spaces everywhere.
Everywhere are sheep.
Sheep are white and fluffy.
Fluffy clouds in the sky.
Sky is many different colours.
Colours from all views.
Views you can see birds.
Birds everywhere.
Everywhere the sun is there.
There's granite glistening under the rocks.
Rocks sharp and jagged.

Leah Bailey (11)
Victoria Road Primary School

It Reminded Me Of Old Times

Upon the moor on a mournful, misty morning
I saw a piece of gritty granite as tall as a mountain.
I saw a waterfall spilling over the luscious, green grass.
I saw rivers cutting meanders.
I saw the moor nursing the baby rivers.

I touched the tall and spiky grass.
I touched the misshapen rocks.
I heard the grass blowing in the wind.
It reminded me of old times.

Natasha Bennett (11)
Victoria Road Primary School

Dartmoor Landscape

From the top of the tallest tor
I sat a fantastic view of the moor.
I touched a bit of gritty granite all dirty and dead.
I heard birds twittering in the sky,
I saw Bronze Age huts all mucky.
I saw big bushes and hay hills.
I saw some rocks rumbling and tumbling.

Dwaine Blaby (10)
Victoria Road Primary School

Tallest Tor

From the top of the tallest tor
I saw a hill that miled across the land.
I saw a deer galloping across the grass.
I saw stands of trees
And foxes walking lazily towards them.
I heard running rivers whisping by.

Shaun Brotherston (10)
Victoria Road Primary School

The Dartmoor Tor

Up on the top of the tallest tor
Tangled rocks tower the moor.
I touched a rock that was sharp as a knife
And if I look down I would see a river
That looks like a snake sliding
Like a block of ice across a table.
The grass was as jade as the green robey
And the top of the tor is like a camel's hump.
The rocks are like an elephant's skin.

Jamie Cook (10)
Victoria Road Primary School

The Diary Of Dartmoor

The water is flowing, the Mica sparkles
The wildlife is living
The grass is boggy, it's quite foggy.

The mountain on the moor
Is taller than the floor.

The birds are flying
The sun is shining.

The horses trouble
And the rocks crumble.

The wall is quite tall
Be careful - it might fall!

William Edney (9)
Victoria Road Primary School

Dartmoor Land

From the top of the tallest tor I said,
'Gritty granite sticking to the stones,
Dartmoor Land, when will you come?'

'When my trees come back and rivers are going faster and
                                                    faster uphill.'

When I left I heard a cow.
Waterfall making bubbles to the brown, deep pools.
Stony edges like pale grey crystals in man-made stone and rocks.
Mossy slushy into sharp, bushy grassland.
I reached to the sky. It was icy.
Smelly swamps given to the Bronze Age who fall in.

Carl Hollyhead (11)
Victoria Road Primary School

Dartmoor

From the top of the tallest tor
I saw gritty granite sticking to stones,
I saw stringy, spiky on slanted hills,
I saw bend, bushy, bristly, sharp rocks,
I touched green, gigantic grasshoppers,
I touched gritty, granite rocks,
I heard slushing, swampy, smelly leaves,
I stood in boggy, swampy mud,
I stood on the gigantic, grey rocks,
I stared at razor-sharp rocks,
I heard cracking concrete from the ground.
So visit this slushy, slimy place.

Kierun Tungate (11)
Victoria Road Primary School

Dartmoor Landscape

Upon the moor on a misty morning,
I saw rocks shaped like sugar cubes,
I saw spiky, slanted grass,
I saw a river flowing freely,
I touched the gritty granite rocks,
I touched the gigantic, jagged grass,
I touched the mica, crystalloid rocks,
I stood on the boggy, swampy grass,
I stood on the gigantic rocks that gleamed,
I stared at the glimmery, gleamy reservoir,
I stared at the water that sparkled,
I stared at the fish swimming and swerving.

Ashton Churchill (11)
Victoria Road Primary School

Dartmoor

Dartmoor is very green
Green is the moss upon jagged rocks
Rocks cracked and broken
Broken rivers coming together
Together to the end of land
Land is the tors
Tors are grey surrounded by grass
Grass and rocks upon Dartmoor
Dartmoor is very cold with views
Views you have never seen before
Before the end of spring
Spring comes once a year.

Antony Tungate (10)
Victoria Road Primary School

Dartmoor

From the top of the tallest tor,
I saw a misty, twisty stream,
I saw rock heaps like petrified pillows,
I touched the gritty granite,
I touched the squidgy mud,
I heard the silence of the moor.

From the top of the tallest tor,
I saw the rocks split,
I saw the wildlife grazing on the grass,
I touched the mossy rocks,
I touched the spiky grass,
I heard the silence of the moor.

Ryan Williams (11)
Victoria Road Primary School

The Dartmoor Views

From the top of tallest tor,
I saw wild ponies grazing on jade-green grass,
I saw the twisting tributary linking lakes together,
I saw the rocks which looked like slanted sugar cubes,
I touched the spiky straw,
I touched the gritty granite,
In the silence I heard the grass bashing together.

George Coulson (10)
Victoria Road Primary School

Reach For The Sky!

I saw how the misty, twisty river ran.
I saw how the sparkling water span.
I laid on the rocks to get a tan.
I touched the spiky rocks and because they were so sharp
I couldn't sit down on them.
I reached for the sky and it was as cold as ice.
I heard the birds whistling so sweetly and softly to themselves.

Samantha McCluskey (11)
Victoria Road Primary School

Dartmoor Landscape

From the top of the tallest tor
I saw a muscular horse with his jagged feet.
I touched the plants but I couldn't believe it.
I saw the stringy landscape as if it was waving at me.
I touched the rocks like giant sugar cubes.
The river was flowing like water in a bathtub.
The wind was blowing like Mother Nature was talking to me.

Luke Barnes (11)
Victoria Road Primary School

Dartmoor Landscape Poem

Up on the tallest tor
Rocks towered the moor but slowly, slipping down the steep hill.
See the wild horses and sheep but don't go too close.
See the rivers flow silent then watch them go violently.
Don't forget before you leave, just say amen.

Corrie Austin (11)
Victoria Road Primary School

Dartmoor

Dartmoor's absolutely magnificent.
Magnificent sunshine glinting down on the landscape.
Landscape covered in bright green grass.
Grass mounts covering the ground.
Ground is slushy and covered with trees.
Trees deep green with owls sitting in the hollow.
Hollow pods with seed ready to start growing.
Growing animals with their parents.
Parents taking us to Dartmoor.
Dartmoor is the best!

Georgina Wellock (10)
Victoria Road Primary School

Dartmoor Landscape

On top of the tallest tor,
I saw the most fantastic view of the moor.
I saw the gritty granite and spiky grass like thorns,
I saw ancient rocks and Bronze Age huts,
I touched the water of the cleanest river.

Jadie McGinnes (10)
Victoria Road Primary School

Dartmoor

The grass is green
Green is the colour of the grass
The grass is sharp
Sharp is the movement of a horse
Horse is an animal at Dartmoor
Dartmoor is gritty and muddy
Muddy means squishy.

Sam Austin (11)
Victoria Road Primary School

Dartmoor

Dartmoor is like a big mound
Mounds are like big rocks
Rocks are like big clouds
Clouds are like fluffy sheep
Sheep are like Dartmoor's guardians
Guardians look after the land
Land in Dartmoor is like a smooth river
Rivers are like lines of silk going through the countryside.

Jake Dell (11)
Victoria Road Primary School

Dartmoor Reflection

Dartmoor is very green,
Green as the grass,
Grass is razor-sharp,
Sharp like pointed rocks,
Rocks are like embedded people in the ground,
Grounds are long and steep,
Steep like little mountains,
Mountains are like hills,
Hills stand out,
Out in a free place where people like to go.

Brendan Sturge (10)
Victoria Road Primary School

Dartmoor Poem!

The waterfalls at Dartmoor
are glistening like the
moonlight.
Moonlight
is like the granite on the
rocks.
Rocks
are jagged and sharp.
Sharp
blades everywhere
around.
Around
the rocks and
back
again.

Jade Victoria Elliott (10)
Victoria Road Primary School

Reflections Of Dartmoor!

Twisting, turning rivers
Rivers rushing through the landscape
Landscape and jagged hills
Hills are like humps on a camel's back
Back to nature
Nature under rocks and granite
Granite glinting under the smooth rivers
Rivers rushing and roaring
Roaring rocks are tumbling
Tumbling grass going around and around
Around the tors sheep eat the tickling grass
Grass is the beautiful views
Views of sharp and sparkling embedded rocks of Dartmoor.

Jasmin Poole (11)
Victoria Road Primary School

Memory Of Dartmoor

Dartmoor is landscape
Landscape like a field
Field of lances in the ground
Ground of mud and sludge
Sludge, wet and marshy
Marshy is the ground near the rivers
Rivers race down the mountains
Mountains are like faces popping up
Up high the wind is like flying ice
Ice is spread in the air
Air is covered in a grey blanket.

Jason Pearson (9)
Victoria Road Primary School

Dartmoor

Dartmoor is covered in rocks
Rocks spread across the grass
Grass like sharp knives
Knives like glinting granite
Granite shining on the ground
Ground slushy like running water
Water as cold as ice!

Jasmin Evans-Viney (9)
Victoria Road Primary School

Dartmoor Trip

Dartmoor has a stunning view
Views embedded in the trees
Trees high in the sky
Sky deep blue with cotton wool clouds
Clouds bright white above the landscape
Landscape stunningly beautiful
Beautiful is Dartmoor.

Elisha Brogan (10)
Victoria Road Primary School

Dartmoor

Dartmoor has a lot of green grass
Grass is like spikes
Spikes are like knives sticking up
Up on the mountain the rocks are jagged
Jagged, glistening rocks
Rocks are granite cracked.

Kyle Matthews (10)
Victoria Road Primary School

Dartmoor

Dartmoor is very green
Green covers the landscape
Landscape flowing far and wide
Wide open spaces everywhere
Everywhere are sheep
Sheep covered in warm wool
Wool looks like the clouds
Clouds float in the sky
Sky is often many colours
Colours fill the world.

Joe Oldham (11)
Victoria Road Primary School

Reflection Of Dartmoor

Dartmoor is like camel humps
Humps like small mountains
Mountains like big muscular rocks
Rocks like jagged teeth
Teeth like granite with lichen
Lichen laying upon rock embedded into the ground
Ground all gritty and murky
Murky ground full of nature.

Jacob William Eyre (11)
Victoria Road Primary School

Dartmoor

Dartmoor, windy and steep
Steep hills rolling down
Down comes the rushing water
Water listening in the waterfall
Waterfall tumbling and crashing onto the rocks
Rocks embedded into the grass
Grass pointed and sharp
Sharp, jagged rocks
Rocks cracked and crumbling
Crumbling mounds glinting bright
Bright sun glaring down at Dartmoor
Dartmoor, beautiful and magnificent.

James Herbert (10)
Victoria Road Primary School

Reflections Of Dartmoor

Dartmoor is very light
Light glistering on the tors
Tors stand out bold and strong
Strong granite boulders covered by lichen
Lichen showing the age of time
Time to gaze upon the sight
Sight of rivers flowing by
By the valley, over the rocks
Rocks shining in the sunlight
Sunlight fading into evening
Evening comes and visitors gone.

Chad Johnson (10)
Victoria Road Primary School

Dartmoor

Dartmoor's kissing the clouds
Clouds forming everywhere
Everywhere green grass
Grass with rocks embedded in ground
Ground wet and slushy
Slushy marshland
Land dotted with jagged rocks
Rocks dotted all over the landscape
Landscape is very wide
Wide and massive skies
Skies with woolly clouds
Clouds above Dartmoor.

Alex J Westmore (11)
Victoria Road Primary School

Spring

Spring come, spring go, flowers bloom,
Snowdrops grow, snowdrops grow, snowdrops grow,
Snowdrops grow!

Birds sing, frogs spring, dew on the grass,
Daffodils grow, daffodils grow, daffodils grow,
Daffodils grow!

Frogspawn in the pond, male frogs croak,
Blossom from the apple trees,
Tulips grow, tulips grow, tulips grow.
Tulips grow!

Frogs mate, shoots peep,
Sun comes up at dawn,
Toads leap, toads leap, toads leap,
Toads leap!

Cushla McDonald (8)
Yealmpton Primary School

I Wish

I wish I was a cheetah,
Speeding around all night,
Catching all the antelope
And giving them a fright.

I wish I was a monkey
Swinging through the trees,
Eating sweet, exotic fruits
And picking others' fleas.

I wish I was an elephant
With a trunk to wave around
And big, heavy feet
To stomp on the ground.

But I'm only a human,
No trunk, no heavy feet,
I am happy with what I am
Without eating antelope meat!

Miranda Heath (8)
Yealmpton Primary School

Something

Last night, while I lay thinking here,
Something funny crawled into my ear.
Then something pranced and partied all night,
What if this something got me in a fight?
What if this something makes me cry?
What if this something makes me lie?
What if this something makes my house go up in flames?
What if this something makes children call me names?
That morning I woke and the what if had gone
I wondered if the whatifs would strike again.

Charlotte Beaumont (8)
Yealmpton Primary School

Spring Timeless

The very light rain falling through the trees
lightly from the delicate sky
and onto the floor.
Spring, timeless spring.
Time, time, timeless.

Daniel Dennis (8)
Yealmpton Primary School

Autumn Come, Autumn Go

Autumn come, autumn go
Lightning bright, thunder loud
Lightning bright, thunder loud
Lightning bright, thunder loud
Lightning bright, thunder loud, loud, loud.

Autumn come, autumn go
Leaves come, leaves go
Munch, crunch,
Munch, crunch,
Munch, crunch,
Munch, crunch, crunch, crunch!

Jack Hooper (8)
Yealmpton Primary School

Monster

Big monster hairy
Small monster spotty
Wide monster scary
Squished monster dotty
Fit monster daring
Jumpy monster silly
Nice monster caring
Lazy monster called Billy!

Scott Magrath (8)
Yealmpton Primary School

I Would Like To Rise And Go

I would like to rise and go
where the juicy apples grow
where under another sky
where stripy tigers lie.

I would like to rise and go
where the pinky blossoms grow and grow
where the greeny rivers flow
where the golden statues glow.

I would like to rise and go
where nobody would ever know
where you could roast marshmallows all night . . .
and where you could only have the fire for light.

Ellie Rogers (9)
Yealmpton Primary School

Winter Come, Winter Go

Winter come, winter go
Oak trees bare
Green frogs stare cold.

Winter come, winter go
Winter cold, winter cold
Winter cold.

Winter come, winter go
Winter crow flies around
Deep, deep snow.

Winter crow
Winter crow
Winter crow.

Charlotte Hendry (8)
Yealmpton Primary School